WORK AND PRAYER

WORK AND PRAYER

COMPILED BY
CHRIS KEATING

morehouse

Morehouse
4775 Linglestown Road
Harrisburg
PA 17112

Continuum
The Tower Building
11 York Road
London SE1 7NX

Morehouse is an imprint of Continuum Books

www.continuumbooks.com

First published 2005

Morning Has Broken by Eleanor Farjeon taken from
The Children's Bells OUP is used with permission

British Library Cataloguing-in-Publication Data
A catalogue record for this book is available from the British Library.

ISBN 0-8192-8121-2

Typeset by RefineCatch Limited, Bungay, Suffolk
Printed and bound by MPG Books Ltd, Bodmin, Cornwall

CONTENTS

FOREWORD BY THE ARCHBISHOP OF CANTERBURY

Daily prayer ought to be a wholly natural activity for all of us – a turning to the sources of our faith for words of praise and insights into our condition, a regular and confident turning to God in honest repentance, a generous turning to the world in compassion and hope.

What Chris Keating's fine book offers is an absolutely straightforward structure with a simple and manageable programme of Biblical reading and a rich use of psalm, hymn and canticle. It gives a framework that can easily be understood and that connects the worshipper with the great tidal currents of shared prayer throughout the Church's history. It is a splendid composition for which I am very grateful, and I warmly commend it to all.

✝ Rowan Cantaur

INTRODUCTION

How do we stay spiritually healthy during a typical working week? How do we stay in touch with God and at the same time lead a busy, and often stressful, demanding working life? In my experience as a parish priest many sincere Christians find it very difficult, and some have given up on it altogether, hardly ever praying or reading their Bibles during the week. Some have a stop/start prayer life, with many resolutions to do better! Not very satisfactory. The answer, however, is quite simple, and has been used since the early days of the Church. It is to plug prayer at regular intervals into the working day. This book is a tool to enable you to do that.

St Benedict of Nursia, sixth century, drew up a rule to regulate the lives of his followers, who were laymen. The rule was based on two activities, *work* and *prayer*. In doing this he was developing earlier rules that Christians had used, but taking out the more extreme austerities. The Psalmist had written, 'Seven times in the day do I praise thee' (Psalm 119.164). And so Benedict's rule was based on seven short times of prayer and praise equally spaced throughout the day. This rule is still used today by the Benedictine Order. What I have done with this book is to reduce and simplify the seven times a day to a more manageable four times a day.

At the time of the Reformation Archbishop Cranmer reduced the seven times a day to twice a day, with his Morning and Evening Prayer in the Book of Common Prayer. It was his hope that lay people would go into church morning and evening for prayer as well as the clergy. His hopes have not been fulfilled, and, what is more, I understand that today many clergy do not say morning and evening prayer. There is a poverty of prayer in the land, and I think that we are all feeling it!

During the Nazi period in Germany the Christian pastor Dietrich Bonhoeffer wrote a book entitled *Gemeinsames Leben* (*Life Together*, 1938) in which he, like Benedict, links prayer and work as belonging together; the one giving identity and meaning to the other:

> Praying and working are two different things. Prayer should not be hindered by work, but neither should work be hindered by prayer. Just as it was God's will that man should work six days and rest and make holy day in his presence on the seventh, so it is also God's will that every day should be marked for the Christian by both prayer and work . . . they belong inseparably together.

How to use this book

Each of the prayer times is reasonably short. Midday prayer and late evening prayer are very compact. Morning and evening prayer have the daily Bible reading tables (the Lectionary) included in them. This you will find at the rear of the book, with Old Testament and New Testament readings for the year, plus a few from the Apocryha. The lectionary readings should be followed where possible, but if time is difficult then the chapter is sufficient. The maximum benefit will be gained if you pray three or four times daily. It is possible to use these forms of prayer with a friend, or in the family. I have not included Sundays in daily prayer as this is when we are all together in church, and at rest with our families and friends.

The Lectionary

I have used Cranmer's original Lectionary, which follows the civil or calendar year, rather than following the church year, because it is much simpler to use, and ensures a continuous reading of scripture throughout the year. The readings for Ash Wednesday, Good Friday, Easter, Ascension, Pentecost and Trinity are in a separate table, and can be used at the appropriate calendar date. As long as we have a variable Easter, with consequent variations in the number of Sundays after Epiphany and after Trinity, that is anywhere from March 22nd to April 25th, this seems to me to be the easiest way to order yearly readings.

The Collects

Because the date of Easter varies from year to year, the number of collects after the Epiphany and after Trinity varies also. I have therefore decided to include all of the collects for the year, excluding saints days etc., at the back of the book. You will need to find out which Sunday of the year it is, or use the collects according to your own choice. Alternatively, you need not use them at all, as there are collects in place in the various times of prayer contained within this book.

I wish you well, and pray that God will give you grace to persevere.

Monday

MORNING PRAYER

Monday

In the name of the Father, and of the Son, and of the
Holy Spirit.
Amen.

The Lord bless us at the beginning of this new week.
May we do, say and think only what pleases Him.

O Lord, open our lips
and our mouths shall proclaim your praise.

**Glory to the Father, and to the Son,
and to the Holy Spirit;
as it was in the beginning, is now,
and shall be for ever. Amen.**

Morning hymn

**Awake, my soul, and with the sun
thy daily stage of duty run;
shake off dull sloth, and joyful rise
to pay thy morning sacrifice.**

**Redeem thy mis-spent time that's past,
and live this day as if thy last;
improve thy talent with due care;
for the great day thyself prepare.**

**Let all thy converse be sincere,
thy conscience as the noon-day clear;
think how all-seeing God thy ways
and all thy secret thoughts surveys.**

**Wake, and lift up thyself, my heart,
and with the angels bear thy part,
who all night long unwearied sing
high praise to the eternal King.**

Psalm 5.3–8

Antiphon: **In the morning, O Lord**

1 In the morning, O Lord, you hear my voice;
  in the morning I lay my requests before you and wait in
    expectation.

2 You are not a God who takes pleasure in evil;
  with you the wicked cannot dwell.

3 The arrogant cannot stand in your presence;
  you hate all who do wrong.

4 You destroy those who tell lies;
  bloodthirsty and deceitful men the Lord abhors.

5 But I, by your great mercy, will come into your house;
  in reverence will I bow down towards your holy temple.

6 Lead me, O Lord, in your righteousness because of my
    enemies;
  make straight your way before me.

Glory to the Father, and to the Son,
and to the Holy Spirit;
as it was in the beginning, is now,
and shall be for ever. Amen.

Antiphon: **In the morning, O Lord, you hear my voice**

Chapter

1 Corinthians 16.13–14

Be on your guard; stand firm in the faith; be men/women of
courage; be strong. Do everything in love.

Thanks be to God.

Lectionary readings – *if you have time,
one or both*

O. T. reading

Psalm 100

1 Shout for joy to the Lord, all the earth.
    Worship the Lord with gladness;
        come before him with joyful songs.

2 Know that the Lord is God.
    It is he who made us, and we are his;
        we are his people, the sheep of his pasture.

3 Enter his gates with thanksgiving
        and his courts with praise;
    give thanks to him and praise his name.

4 For the Lord is good and his love endures for ever;
    his faithfulness continues through all generations.

**Glory to the Father, and to the Son,
and to the Holy Spirit;
as it was in the beginning, is now,
and shall be for ever. Amen.**

N. T. reading

Canticle

Micah 6.6–8

Antiphon: **With what shall I come**

1 With what shall I come before the Lord
    and bow down before the exalted God?
  Shall I come before him with burnt offerings,
    with calves a year old?

2 Will the Lord be pleased with thousands of rams,
  with ten thousand rivers of oil?

3 Shall I offer my firstborn for my transgression,
  the fruit of my body for the sin of my soul?

4 He has showed you, O man, what is good.
  And what does the Lord require of you?

5 To act justly and to love mercy
  and to walk humbly with your God.

Glory to the Father, and to the Son,
and to the Holy Spirit;
as it was in the beginning, is now,
and shall be for ever. Amen.

Antiphon: **With what shall I come before the Lord**

The Prayers

The Kyries

Lord, have mercy.
Christ, have mercy.
Lord, have mercy.

The Lord's Prayer

Our Father in heaven,
hallowed be your name,
your kingdom come,
your will be done,
on earth as in heaven.
Give us today our daily bread.
Forgive us our sins
as we forgive those who sin against us.
Lead us not into temptation
but deliver us from evil.
[For the kingdom, the power,
and the glory are yours
now and for ever.] Amen.

O Lord, arise, help us
and deliver us for your name's sake.

Turn us again, O Lord God of hosts.
Show the light of your countenance, and we shall be whole.

O Lord, hear our prayer
and let our cry come to you.

The Collect of the day, or the following:

Almighty God,
who sent your Holy Spirit
to be the life and light of your Church:
open our hearts to the riches of your grace,
that we may bring forth the fruit of the Spirit
in love and joy and peace;
through Jesus Christ our Lord.
Amen.

Silent prayer

Conclusion

The Lord be with you
and with your spirit.

Let us bless the Lord.
Thanks be to God.

The grace of our Lord Jesus Christ,
and the love of God,
and the fellowship of the Holy Spirit,
be with us all evermore.
Amen.

MIDDAY PRAYER

Monday

O God, make speed to save us.
O Lord, make haste to help us.

Glory to the Father, and to the Son,
and to the Holy Spirit;
as it was in the beginning, is now,
and shall be for ever. Amen.

Hymn

Come, Holy Spirit, ever One
with God the Father and the Son:
come swiftly, fount of grace, and pour
into our hearts your boundless store.

With all our strength, with heart and tongue,
by word and deed your praise be sung:
and love light up our mortal frame
till others catch the living flame.

O Father, that we ask be done
through Jesus Christ, your only Son,
who, with the Spirit, reigns above;
three persons in one God of love.
Amen.

Psalm 119.33–48

Antiphon: **Teach me, O Lord**

1 Teach me, O Lord, to follow your decrees;
   then I will keep them to the end.

2 Give me understanding, and I will keep your law
   and obey it with all my heart.

3 Direct me in the path of your commands,
   for there I find delight.

4 Turn my heart towards your statutes
   and not towards selfish gain.

5 Turn my eyes away from worthless things;
   preserve my life according to your word.

6 Fulfil your promise to your servant,
   so that you may be feared.

7 Take away the disgrace I dread,
   for your laws are good.

8 How I long for your precepts!
   Preserve my life in your righteousness.

9 May your unfailing love come to me, O Lord,
   your salvation according to your promise.

10 Then I will answer the one who taunts me,
   for I trust in your word.

11 Do not snatch the word of truth from my mouth,
   for I have put my hope in your laws.

12 I will always obey your law,
   for ever and ever.

13 I will walk about in freedom,
   for I have sought out your precepts.

14 I will speak of your statutes before kings
   and will not be put to shame.

15 For I delight in your commands
because I love them.

16 I lift up my hands to your commands, which I love,
and I meditate on your decrees.

Glory to the Father, and to the Son,
and to the Holy Spirit;
as it was in the beginning, is now,
and shall be for ever. Amen.

Antiphon: **Teach me, O Lord, to follow your decrees**

Chapter
Ephesians 4.1–6

As a prisoner for the Lord, then, I urge you to live a life
worthy of the calling you have received. Be completely
humble and gentle; be patient, bearing with one another
in love. Make every effort to keep the unity of the Spirit
through the bond of peace. There is one body and one
Spirit – just as you were called to one hope when you were
called – one Lord, one faith, one baptism; one God and
Father of all, who is over all and through all and in all.

Thanks be to God.

Canticle

Isaiah 12.1–6

Antiphon: **Although you were angry**

1 In that day you will say:
    'I will praise you, O Lord.
  Although you were angry with me,
    your anger has turned away
    and you have comforted me.

2 Surely God is my salvation;
    I will trust and not be afraid.
  The Lord, the Lord, is my strength and my song;
    he has become my salvation.'

3 With joy you will draw water
    from the wells of salvation.

4 In that day you will say:
    'Give thanks to the Lord, call on his name;
  make known among the nations what he has done,
    and proclaim that his name is exalted.

5 Sing to the Lord, for he has done glorious things;
    let this be known to all the world.

6 Shout aloud and sing for joy, people of Zion,
    for great is the Holy One of Israel among you.'

Antiphon: **Although you were angry with me, your anger has turned away**

The Prayers

The Kyries

Lord, have mercy.
Christ, have mercy.
Lord, have mercy.

The Lord's Prayer

Our Father in heaven,
hallowed be your name,
your kingdom come,
your will be done,
on earth as in heaven.
Give us today our daily bread.
Forgive us our sins
as we forgive those who sin against us.
Lead us not into temptation
but deliver us from evil.
[For the kingdom, the power,
and the glory are yours
now and for ever.] Amen.

Let your merciful kindness, O Lord, be upon us,
as we do put our trust in you.

Let your priests be clothed with righteousness
and your people sing with joyfulness.

O Lord, save our nation
and mercifully hear us when we call upon you.

O God, save your people,
who put their trust in you.

The Collect of the day, or the following:

God in heaven,
may your Holy Spirit,
the comforter who proceeds from you,
enlighten our minds,
lead us into all truth
and make us active in your service;
through Jesus Christ our Lord.
Amen.

Conclusion

O Lord, hear our prayer
and let our cry come to you.

Let us bless the Lord.
Thanks be to God.

May God kindle in us the fire of love.
Amen.

EVENING PRAYER

Monday

O Lord, open our lips
and our mouth shall proclaim your praise.

Let us worship the Lord.
All praise to his name.

**Glory to the Father, and to the Son,
and to the Holy Spirit;
as it was in the beginning, is now,
and shall be for ever. Amen.**

Evening hymn

**O blest Creator of the light,
who mak'st the day with radiance bright,
and o'er the forming world didst call
the light from chaos first of all.**

**Whose wisdom join'd in meet array
the morn and eve, and nam'd them day:
night comes with all its darkling fears
regards thy people's prayers and tears.**

**Lest, sunk in sin, and whelm'd with strife,
they lose the gift of endless life;
while, thinking but the thoughts of time,
they weave new chains of woe and crime.**

**But grant them grace that they may strain
the heav'nly gate and prize to gain;
each harmful lure aside to cast,
and purge away each error past.**

Psalm 141

Antiphon: **May my prayer**

1 O Lord, I call to you; come quickly to me.
   Hear my voice when I call to you.

2 May my prayer be set before you like incense;
   may the lifting up of my hands be like the evening
      sacrifice.

3 Set a guard over my mouth, O Lord;
   keep watch over the door of my lips.

4 Let not my heart be drawn to what is evil,
   to take part in wicked deeds with men who are evildoers;
      let me not eat of their delicacies.

5 Let a righteous man strike me – it is a kindness;
      let him rebuke me – it is oil on my head.
   My head will not refuse it.
   Yet my prayer is ever against the deeds of evildoers.

6 Their rulers will be thrown down from the cliffs,
   and the wicked will learn that my words were well
      spoken.

7 They will say, 'As one ploughs and breaks up the earth,
   so our bones have been scattered at the mouth of the
      grave.'

8 But my eyes are fixed on you, O Sovereign Lord;
   in you I take refuge; do not give me over to death.

9 Keep me from the snares they have laid for me,
   from the traps set by evildoers.

10 Let the wicked fall into their own nets,
   while I pass by in safety.

Glory to the Father, and to the Son,
and to the Holy Spirit;
as it was in the beginning, is now,
and shall be for ever. Amen.

Antiphon: **May my prayer be set before you like incense**

Chapter
2 Thessalonians 3.5

May the Lord direct your hearts into God's love and
Christ's perseverance.

Thanks be to God.

Lectionary readings – if you have time, one or both

O. T. reading

Magnificat – The Song of Mary
Luke 1.46–55

Antiphon: **My soul proclaims**

1 My soul proclaims the greatness of the Lord;
   my spirit rejoices in God my Saviour.

2 For he has looked with favour on his lowly servant;
   from this day all generations will call me blessed.

3 The Almighty has done great things for me,
   and holy is his name.

4 He has mercy on those who fear him
   in every generation.

5 He has shown the strength of his arm;
   he has scattered the proud in their conceit.

6 He has cast down the mighty from their thrones
   and has lifted up the lowly.

7 He has filled the hungry with good things
   and the rich he has sent away empty.

8 He has come to the help of his servant, Israel,
   for he has remembered his promise of mercy.

9 The promise he made to our forebears,
   to Abraham and his children for ever.

**Glory to the Father, and to the Son,
and to the Holy Spirit;
as it was in the beginning, is now,
and shall be for ever. Amen.**

Antiphon: **My soul proclaims the greatness of the Lord**

N. T. reading

The Prayers

Let my prayer come before you, O Lord.
The lifting of my hands like the evening sacrifice.

The Kyries

Lord, have mercy.
Christ, have mercy.
Lord, have mercy.

The Lord's Prayer

Our Father in heaven,
hallowed be your name,
your kingdom come,
your will be done,
on earth as in heaven.
Give us today our daily bread.
Forgive us our sins
as we forgive those who sin against us.
Lead us not into temptation
but deliver us from evil.
[For the kingdom, the power,
and the glory are yours
now and for ever.] Amen.

I said Lord be merciful to me.
Heal my soul because I have sinned against you.

Turn again, O Lord, at the last
and be gracious to your servants.

Let your merciful kindness be upon us,
for we put our trust in you.

Let your priests be clothed with righteousness
and your people sing with joyfulness.

O Lord, save our nation
and teach those who govern us wisdom.

Give your people the blessing of peace
and let your rule extend over all the earth.

Make our hearts clean, O God,
and renew a right Spirit within us.

O Lord, hear our prayer
and let our cry come to you.

The Collect of the day, or the following:

Lord, you have taught us
that all our doings without love are nothing worth;
send your Holy Spirit
and pour into our hearts that most excellent gift of love,
the true bond of peace and of all virtues,
without which whoever lives is counted dead before you.
Grant this for the sake of your only Son,
Jesus Christ our Lord.
Amen.

Silent prayer

Conclusion

The grace of our Lord Jesus Christ,
and the love of God,
and the fellowship of the Holy Spirit,
be with us all evermore.
Amen.

Let us bless the Lord.
Thanks be to God.

AN ORDER FOR COMPLINE
(A Late Evening Service)

Monday

The Lord Almighty grant us a quiet night and a perfect end.
Amen.

Be self-controlled and alert. Your enemy the devil prowls
around like a roaring lion looking for someone to devour.
Resist him, standing firm in the faith.

(1 Peter 5.8–9)

But you, O Lord, have mercy upon us.
Thanks be to God.

O God, make speed to save us.
O Lord, make haste to help us.

**Glory to the Father, and to the Son,
and to the Holy Spirit;
as it was in the beginning, is now,
and shall be for ever. Amen.**

Praise to the Lord.
The Lord's name be praised.

Psalm 4

1 Answer me when I call, O God of my righteousness;
  you set me at liberty when I was in trouble;
    have mercy on me and hear my prayer.

2 How long will you nobles dishonour my glory;
  how long will you love vain things and seek after
       falsehood?

3 But know that the Lord has shown me his marvellous
       kindness;
  when I call upon the Lord, he will hear me.

4 Stand in awe, and sin not;
  commune with your own heart upon your bed, and be
       still.

5 Offer the sacrifices of righteousness
  and put your trust in the Lord.

6 There are many that say, 'Who will show us any good?'
  Lord, lift up the light of your countenance upon us.

7 You have put gladness in my heart,
  more than when their corn and wine and oil increase.

8 In peace I will lie down and sleep,
  for it is you Lord, only, who make me dwell in safety.

Short lesson

You, O Lord, are in the midst of us, and we are called by
your name. Leave us not, O Lord our God.

(Jeremiah 14.9)

Work and Prayer

Hymn

Before the ending of the day,
Creator of the world, we pray:
protect us by your mighty grace,
grant us your mercy and your peace.

Bless us in sleep, that we may find
no terrors to disturb our mind;
our cunning enemy restrain –
guard us from sin and all its stain.

O Father, may your will be done
through Jesus Christ your only Son;
whom with the Spirit we adore,
one God, both now and evermore.

Antiphon: Preserve us, O Lord, while waking, and guard us
while sleeping, that awake we may watch with Christ, and
asleep we may rest in peace.

The Prayers

The Kyries

Lord, have mercy.
Christ, have mercy.
Lord, have mercy.

The Lord's Prayer

Our Father in heaven,
hallowed be your name,
your kingdom come,
your will be done,
on earth as in heaven.
Give us today our daily bread.
Forgive us our sins
as we forgive those who sin against us.
Lead us not into temptation
but deliver us from evil.
[For the kingdom, the power,
and the glory are yours
now and for ever.] Amen.

I will bless the Lord who has given me counsel,
and in the night watches he instructs my heart.

I have set the Lord always before me.
He is at my right hand; I shall not fall.

Weigh my heart, examine me by night.
Refine me, and you will find no impurity in me.

We confess to God Almighty,
the Father, the Son, and the Holy Spirit,
that we have sinned in thought, word, and deed,
through our own grievous fault.
Therefore we pray God to have mercy upon us.

Almighty God, have mercy upon us,
forgive us all our sins and deliver us from all evil,
confirm and strengthen us in all goodness,
and bring us to life everlasting;
through Jesus Christ our Lord.
Amen.

Will you not give us life again, O Lord:
that your people may rejoice in you?

Show us your mercy, O Lord,
and grant us your salvation.

Keep us tonight, Lord, from all sin.
Have mercy on us, Lord, have mercy.

Lord, hear our prayer
and let our cry come to you.

Collect

Visit this place, O Lord we pray,
and drive from it all the snares of the enemy;
let your holy angels dwell herein to preserve us in peace;
and may your blessing be upon us evermore;
through Jesus Christ our Lord.
Amen.

Nunc Dimittis

1 Now, Lord, you let your servant go in peace:
   your word has been fulfilled.

2 My own eyes have seen the salvation
   which you have prepared in the sight of every people:

3 A light to reveal you to the nations
   and the glory of your people Israel.

**Glory to the Father, and to the Son,
and to the Holy Spirit;
as it was in the beginning, is now,
and shall be for ever. Amen.**

We will lay us down in peace and take our rest,
for it is you, Lord, only who make us dwell in safety.

The Lord be with you
and with your spirit.

Let us bless the Lord.
Thanks be to God.

**The Almighty and merciful Lord,
the Father, the Son, and the Holy Spirit,
bless and preserve us. Amen.**

Tuesday

MORNING PRAYER

Tuesday

In the name of the Father, and of the Son, and of the Holy Spirit.
Amen.

The Lord is high above all people.
And his glory above the heaven.

O God, make speed to save us.
O Lord, make haste to help us.

Glory to the Father, and to the Son,
and to the Holy Spirit;
as it was in the beginning, is now,
and shall be for ever. Amen.

Morning hymn

A brighter dawn is breaking,
and earth with praise is waking;
for thou, O King most highest,
the pow'r of death defiest.

And thou hast come victorious,
with risen body glorious,
who now for ever livest,
and life abundant givest.

O free the world from blindness,
and fill the earth with kindness,
give sinners resurrection,
bring striving to perfection.

In sickness give us healing,
in doubt thy clear revealing,
that praise to thee be given
in earth as in thy heaven.

Psalm 63.1–8

Antiphon: **O God, you are my God**

1 O God, you are my God; eagerly I seek you;
  my soul is athirst for you.

2 My flesh also faints for you,
  as in a dry and thirsty land where there is no water.

3 So would I gaze upon you in your holy place,
  that I might behold your power and your glory.

4 Your loving-kindness is better than life itself
  and so my lips shall praise you.

5 I will bless you as long as I live
  and lift up my hands in your name.

6 My soul shall be satisfied, as with marrow and fatness,
  and my mouth shall praise you with joyful lips,

7 When I remember you upon my bed
  and meditate on you in the watches of the night.

8 For you have been my helper
  and under the shadow of your wings will I rejoice.

Glory to the Father, and to the Son,
and to the Holy Spirit;
as it was in the beginning, is now,
and shall be for ever. Amen.

Antiphon: **O God, you are my God; eagerly I seek you**

Chapter

1 Thessalonians 5.16–18

Be joyful always, pray continually; give thanks in all circumstances, for this is God's will for you in Christ Jesus.

Thanks be to God.

Lectionary readings – if you have time, one or both

O. T. reading

Psalm 15

1 Lord, who may dwell in your tabernacle?
   Who may rest upon your holy hill?

2 Whoever leads an uncorrupt life
   and does the thing that is right;

3 Who speaks the truth from the heart
   and bears no deceit on the tongue;

4 Who does no evil to a friend
   and pours no scorn on a neighbour;

5 In whose sight the wicked are not esteemed,
   but who honours those who fear the Lord.

6 Whoever has sworn to a neighbour
   and never goes back on that word;

7 Who does not lend money in hope of gain,
   nor takes a bribe against the innocent;

8 Whoever does these things
   shall never fall.

**Glory to the Father, and to the Son,
and to the Holy Spirit;
as it was in the beginning, is now,
and shall be for ever. Amen.**

N. T. reading

Canticle

1 Chronicles 29.10–14

Antiphon: **Praise be to you**

1 David praised the Lord
    in the presence of the whole assembly,
    saying,
  'Praise be to you, O Lord,
    God of our Father Israel,
    from everlasting to everlasting.

2 Yours, O Lord, is the greatness and the power
    and the glory and the majesty and the splendour,
    for everything in heaven and earth is yours.
  Yours, O Lord, is the kingdom;
    you are exalted as head over all.

3 Wealth and honour come from you;
    you are the ruler of all things.
  In your hands are strength and power
    to exalt and give strength to all.

4 Now, our God, we give you thanks,
  and praise your glorious name.

5 But who am I, and who are my people,
    that we should be able to give as generously as this?
  Everything comes from you,
    and we have given you only what comes from your
      hand.'

Glory to the Father, and to the Son,
and to the Holy Spirit;
as it was in the beginning, is now,
and shall be for ever. Amen.

Antiphon: **Praise be to you, O Lord**

The Prayers

The Kyries

Lord, have mercy.
Christ, have mercy.
Lord, have mercy.

The Lord's Prayer

**Our Father in heaven,
hallowed be your name,
your kingdom come,
your will be done,
on earth as in heaven.
Give us today our daily bread.
Forgive us our sins
as we forgive those who sin against us.
Lead us not into temptation
but deliver us from evil.
[For the kingdom, the power,
    and the glory are yours
now and for ever.] Amen.**

The Lord is high above all,
and his glory above the heavens.

Have I not thought of you when I was waking,
because you have been my helper?

O Lord, hear our prayer
and let our cry come to you.

The Collect of the day, or the following:

Eternal God and Father,
you create us by your power
and redeem us by your love:
guide and strengthen us by your Spirit
that we may give ourselves in love and service
to one another and to you;
through Jesus Christ our Lord.
Amen.

Silent prayer

Conclusion

The Lord be with you
and with your spirit.

Let us bless the Lord.
Thanks be to God.

The Lord bless and watch over us during this day, and give
us his wisdom.
Amen.

MIDDAY PRAYER

Tuesday

O God, make speed to save us.
O Lord, make haste to help us.

**Glory to the Father, and to the Son,
and to the Holy Spirit;
as it was in the beginning, is now,
and shall be for ever. Amen.**

Hymn

**As pants the hart for cooling streams
when heated in the chase,
so longs my soul, O God, for thee,
and thy refreshing grace.**

**For thee, my God, the living God,
my thirsty soul doth pine:
O when shall I behold thy face,
thou majesty divine?**

**Why restless, why cast down, my soul?
hope still, and thou shall sing
the praise, of him who is thy God,
thy health's eternal spring.**

**To Father, Son and Holy Ghost,
the God whom we adore,
be glory, as it was, is now,
and shall be evermore.**

Psalm 119.97–104

Antiphon: **Oh, how I love**

1 Lord, how I love your law!
   All the day long it is my study.

2 Your commandments have made me wiser than my
         enemies,
   for they are ever with me.

3 I have more understanding than all my teachers,
   for your testimonies are my meditation.

4 I am wiser than the aged,
   because I keep your commandments.

5 I restrain my feet from every evil way,
   that I may keep your word.

6 I have not turned aside from your judgements,
   for you have been my teacher.

7 How sweet are your words on my tongue!
   They are sweeter than honey to my mouth.

8 Through your commandments I get understanding;
   therefore I hate all lying ways.

Glory to the Father, and to the Son,
and to the Holy Spirit;
as it was in the beginning, is now,
and shall be for ever. Amen.

Antiphon: **Oh, how I love your law**

Chapter

Hebrews 12.7–11

Endure hardship as discipline; God is treating you as sons. For what Son is not disciplined by his Father? If you are not disciplined (and everyone undergoes discipline), then you are illegitimate children and not true sons. Moreover, we have all had human fathers who disciplined us and we respected them for it. How much more should we submit to the Father of our spirits and live! Our fathers disciplined us for a little while as they thought best; but God disciplines us for our good, that we may share in his holiness. No discipline seems pleasant at the time, but painful. Later on, however, it produces a harvest of righteousness and peace for those who have been trained by it.

Thanks be to God.

Canticle

Isaiah 55.6–11

Antiphon: **Seek the Lord**

1 Seek the Lord while he may be found,
   call on him while he is near.

2 Let the wicked forsake his way
      and the evil man his thoughts.
   Let him turn to the Lord,
      and he will have mercy on him,
      and to our God, for he will freely pardon.

3 'For my thoughts are not your thoughts,
   neither are your ways my ways.'

4 'As the heavens are higher than the earth,
   so are my ways higher than your ways
      and my thoughts than your thoughts.

5 As the rain and snow come down from heaven,
   and do not return to it without watering the earth
      and making it bud and flourish,
         so that it yields seed for the sower and bread for the
            eater,

6 So is my word that goes out from my mouth:
   It will not return to me empty
      but will accomplish what I desire
      and achieve the purpose for which I sent it.'

Antiphon: **Seek the Lord while he may be found**

The Prayers

The Kyries

Lord, have mercy.
Christ, have mercy.
Lord, have mercy.

The Lord's Prayer

Our Father in heaven,
hallowed be your name,
your kingdom come,
your will be done,
on earth as in heaven.
Give us today our daily bread.
Forgive us our sins
as we forgive those who sin against us.
Lead us not into temptation
but deliver us from evil.
[For the kingdom, the power,
and the glory are yours
now and for ever.] Amen.

Hear my voice, O Lord, when I call.
Have mercy on me and answer me.

Teach me your way, O Lord.
Lead me on a level path.

My heart tells of your word, 'Seek my face.'
Your face, Lord, will I seek.

The Collect of the day, or the following:

O God, who for our redemption
willed that your Son
should suffer the death of the cross,
to deliver us from the power of the enemy:
grant to us your servants
that we may always live in the joy of his resurrection;
through Jesus Christ our Lord.
Amen.

Conclusion

O Lord, hear our prayer
and let our cry come to you.

Let us bless the Lord.
Thanks be to God.

May God make us gentle and strong in love.
Amen.

EVENING PRAYER

Tuesday

O Lord, open our lips
and our mouth shall proclaim your praise.

Let us worship the Lord.
All praise to his name.

**Glory to the Father, and to the Son,
and to the Holy Spirit;
as it was in the beginning, is now,
and shall be for ever. Amen.**

Evening hymn

**Hail, gladdening Light, of his pure glory poured,
who is the immortal Father, heavenly, blessed,
Holiest of holies, Jesus Christ our Lord.**

**Now we are come to the sun's hour of rest;
the lights of evening round us shine;
we hymn the Father, Son and Holy Spirit divine.**

**Worthiest art you at all times to be sung
with uncorrupted tongue,
Son of our God, giver of life, alone;
therefore in all the world we make your glories known.**

Psalm 36

1 Sin whispers to the wicked, in the depths of their heart;
 there is no fear of God before their eyes.

2 They flatter themselves in their own eyes
 that their abominable sin will not be found out.

3 The words of their mouth are unrighteous and full of
 deceit;
 they have ceased to act wisely and to do good.

4 They think out mischief upon their beds
 and have set themselves in no good way;
 nor do they abhor that which is evil.

5 Your love, O Lord, reaches to the heavens
 and your faithfulness to the clouds.

6 Your righteousness stands like the strong mountains,
 your justice like the great deep;
 you, Lord, shall save both man and beast.

7 How precious is your loving mercy, O God!
 All mortal flesh shall take refuge
 under the shadow of your wings.

8 They shall be satisfied with the abundance of your
 house;
 they shall drink from the river of your delights.

9 For with you is the well of life
 and in your light shall we see light.

10 O continue your loving-kindness to those who know you
 and your righteousness to those who are true of heart.

11 Let not the foot of pride come against me,
 nor the hand of the ungodly thrust me away.

12 There are they fallen, all who work wickedness.
 They are cast down and shall not be able to stand.

**Glory to the Father, and to the Son,
and to the Holy Spirit;
as it was in the beginning, is now,
and shall be for ever. Amen.**

Antiphon: **Your love, O Lord, reaches to the heavens**

Chapter
Ephesians 1.15–17

For this reason, ever since I heard about your faith in the
Lord Jesus and your love for all the saints, I have not
stopped giving thanks for you, remembering you in my
prayers. I keep asking that the God of our Lord Jesus Christ,
the glorious Father, may give you the Spirit of wisdom and
revelation, so that you may know him better.

Thanks be to God.

Lectionary readings – if you have time, one or both

O. T. reading

Magnificat – The Song of Mary
Luke 1.46–55

Antiphon: **For he has looked with favour**

1 My soul proclaims the greatness of the Lord;
my spirit rejoices in God my Saviour.

2 For he has looked with favour on his lowly servant;
from this day all generations will call me blessed.

3 The Almighty has done great things for me,
and holy is his name.

4 He has mercy on those who fear him
in every generation.

5 He has shown the strength of his arm;
he has scattered the proud in their conceit.

6 He has cast down the mighty from their thrones
and has lifted up the lowly.

7 He has filled the hungry with good things
and the rich he has sent away empty.

8 He has come to the help of his servant, Israel,
for he has remembered his promise of mercy.

9 The promise he made to our forebears,
to Abraham and his children for ever.

**Glory to the Father, and to the Son,
and to the Holy Spirit;
as it was in the beginning, is now,
and shall be for ever. Amen.**

Antiphon: **For he has looked with favour on his lowly servant**

N. T. reading

The Prayers

Your love, O Lord, reaches to the heavens
and your faithfulness to the clouds.

The Kyries

Lord, have mercy.
Christ, have mercy.
Lord, have mercy.

The Lord's Prayer

Our Father in heaven,
hallowed be your name,
your kingdom come,
your will be done,
on earth as in heaven.
Give us today our daily bread.
Forgive us our sins
as we forgive those who sin against us.
Lead us not into temptation
but deliver us from evil.
[For the kingdom, the power,
and the glory are yours
now and for ever.] Amen.

O Lord, arise, help us
and deliver us for your name's sake.

Turn again, O Lord God of hosts.
Show the light of your countenance, and we shall be whole.

O Lord, hear our prayer.
Answer us when we call.

The Collect of the day, or the following:

We beseech you Lord,
pour your grace into our hearts;
that as we have known your Son
by the preaching of the word,
so by his Cross and Passion
we may know the power of his resurrection;
through the same Christ our Lord.
Amen.

Silent prayer

Conclusion

O Lord, hear our prayer
and let our cry come to you.

Let us bless the Lord.
Thanks be to God.

May God in his infinite love keep us in eternal life.
Amen.

AN ORDER FOR COMPLINE
(A Late Evening Service)

Tuesday

The Lord Almighty grant us a quiet night and a perfect end.
Amen.

Be self-controlled and alert. Your enemy the devil prowls
around like a roaring lion looking for someone to devour.
Resist him, standing firm in the faith.

(1 Peter 5.8–9)

But you, O Lord, have mercy upon us.
Thanks be to God.

O God, make speed to save us.
O Lord, make haste to help us.

**Glory to the Father, and to the Son,
and to the Holy Spirit;
as it was in the beginning, is now,
and shall be for ever. Amen.**

Praise to the Lord.
The Lord's name be praised.

Psalm 31.1–5

1 In you, O Lord, have I taken refuge;
   let me never be put to shame;
 deliver me in your righteousness.

2 Incline your ear to me;
 make haste to deliver me.

3 Be my strong rock, a fortress to save me,
   for you are my rock and my stronghold;
 guide me, and lead me for your name's sake.

4 Take me out of the net
   that they have laid secretly for me,
 for you are my strength.

5 Into your hands I commend my spirit,
 for you have redeemed me, O Lord God of truth.

Short lesson

Once, having been asked by the Pharisees when the kingdom
of God would come, Jesus replied, 'The kingdom of God
does not come with your careful observation, nor will people
say, "Here it is," or "There it is," because the kingdom of
God is within you.'

(Luke 17.20–21)

Hymn

Almighty Lord, the holy One
whose reign in glory we await:
look down from your eternal throne
and our dark world illuminate;
from sons and daughters of the light
dispel the shameful deeds of night.

Defend us from all evil powers;
our weakness and fatigue replace
through all the silent sleeping hours
with sweet refreshing by your grace;
forgive our sins, our hope renew,
that we may rest and rise with you.

Antiphon: **Preserve us, O Lord, while waking, and guard us while sleeping, that awake we may watch with Christ, and asleep we may rest in peace.**

The Prayers

The Kyries

Lord, have mercy.
Christ, have mercy.
Lord, have mercy.

The Lord's Prayer

Our Father in heaven,
hallowed be your name,
your kingdom come,
your will be done,
on earth as in heaven.
Give us today our daily bread.
Forgive us our sins
as we forgive those who sin against us.
Lead us not into temptation
but deliver us from evil.
[For the kingdom, the power,
and the glory are yours
now and for ever.] Amen.

I will bless the Lord who has given me counsel,
and in the night watches he instructs my heart.

I have set the Lord always before me.
He is at my right hand; I shall not fall.
Weigh my heart, examine me by night.

Refine me, and you will find no impurity in me.

We confess to God Almighty,
the Father, the Son, and the Holy Spirit,
that we have sinned in thought, word, and deed,
through our own grievous fault.
Therefore we pray God to have mercy upon us.

Almighty God, have mercy upon us,
forgive us all our sins and deliver us from all evil,
confirm and strengthen us in all goodness,
and bring us to life everlasting;
through Jesus Christ our Lord.
Amen.

Will you not give us life again, O Lord:
that your people may rejoice in you?

Show us your mercy, O Lord,
and grant us your salvation.

Keep us tonight, Lord, from all sin.
Have mercy on us, Lord, have mercy.

Lord, hear our prayer
and let our cry come to you.

Collect

Lighten our darkness, Lord, we pray;
and in your mercy
defend us from all perils and dangers of this night;
for the love of your only Son,
our Saviour Jesus Christ.
Amen.

Nunc Dimittis

1 Now, Lord, you let your servant go in peace:
   your word has been fulfilled.

2 My own eyes have seen the salvation
   which you have prepared in the sight of every people:

3 A light to reveal you to the nations
   and the glory of your people Israel.

Glory to the Father, and to the Son,
and to the Holy Spirit;
as it was in the beginning, is now,
and shall be for ever. Amen.

We will lay us down in peace and take our rest,
for it is you, Lord, only who make us dwell in safety.

The Lord be with you
and with your spirit.

Let us bless the Lord.
Thanks be to God.

**The Almighty and merciful Lord,
the Father, the Son, and the Holy Spirit,
bless and preserve us. Amen.**

Wednesday

MORNING PRAYER

Wednesday

In the name of the Father, and of the Son, and of the
  Holy Spirit.
Amen.

Let your merciful kindness, Lord, be upon us,
as we do put our trust in you.

O God, make speed to save us.
O Lord, make haste to help us.

**Glory to the Father, and to the Son,
and to the Holy Spirit;
as it was in the beginning, is now,
and shall be for ever. Amen.**

Morning hymn

**My Father, for another night
of quiet sleep and rest;
for all the joy of morning light,
your holy name be blessed.**

**Now with the new-born day I give
myself to you again;
that gladly I for you may live,
and you within me reign.**

**In every action, great or small,
in every thought and aim;
your glory may I seek in all,
do all in Jesus' name.**

**My Father, for his sake, I pray,
your child accept and bless;
and lead me by your grace today
in paths of righteousness.**

Psalm 8

Antiphon: **When I consider**

1 O Lord our governor,
   how glorious is your name in all the world!

2 Your majesty above the heavens is praised
   out of the mouths of babes at the breast.

3 You have founded a stronghold against your foes,
   that you might still the enemy and the avenger.

4 When I consider your heavens, the work of your fingers,
   the moon and the stars that you have ordained,

5 What are mortals, that you should be mindful of them;
   mere human beings, that you should seek them out?

6 You have made them little lower than the angels
   and crown them with glory and honour.

7 You have given them dominion over the works of your
          hands
   and put all things under their feet,

8 All sheep and oxen,
   even the wild beasts of the field,

9 The birds of the air, the fish of the sea
   and whatsoever moves in the paths of the sea.

10 O Lord our governor,
   how glorious is your name in all the world!

**Glory to the Father, and to the Son,
and to the Holy Spirit;
as it was in the beginning, is now,
and shall be for ever. Amen.**

Antiphon: **When I consider your heavens**

Chapter

Hebrews 3.12–13

See to it brothers/sisters, that none of you has a sinful, unbelieving heart that turns away from the living God. But encourage one another daily, as long as it is called Today, so that none of you may be hardened by sin's deceitfulness.

Thanks be to God.

Lectionary readings – if you have time, one or both

O. T. reading

Psalm 119.73–77

1 Your hands have made me and fashioned me;
   give me understanding, that I may learn your
      commandments.

2 Those who fear you will be glad when they see me,
   because I have hoped in your word.

3 I know, O Lord, that your judgements are right,
   and that in very faithfulness you caused me to be
      troubled.

4 Let your faithful love be my comfort,
   according to your promise to your servant.

5 Let your tender mercies come to me, that I may live,
   for your law is my delight.

**Glory to the Father, and to the Son,
and to the Holy Spirit;
as it was in the beginning, is now,
and shall be for ever. Amen.**

N. T. reading

Canticle
Revelation 15.3–4

Antiphon: **Great and wonderful**

1 Great and wonderful are your deeds,
   Lord God the Almighty.

2 Just and true are your ways,
   O ruler of the nations.

3 Who shall not revere and praise your name, O Lord?
   For you alone are holy.

4 All nations shall come and worship in your presence:
   for your just dealings have been revealed.

Glory to the Father, and to the Son,
and to the Holy Spirit;
as it was in the beginning, is now,
and shall be for ever. Amen.

Antiphon: **Great and wonderful are your deeds**

The Prayers

The Kyries

Lord, have mercy.
Christ, have mercy.
Lord, have mercy.

The Lord's Prayer

Our Father in heaven,
hallowed be your name,
your kingdom come,
your will be done,
on earth as in heaven.
Give us today our daily bread.
Forgive us our sins
as we forgive those who sin against us.
Lead us not into temptation
but deliver us from evil.
[For the kingdom, the power,
and the glory are yours
now and for ever.] Amen.

O Lord, arise, help us
and deliver us for your name's sake.

Turn us again, O Lord of hosts.
Show the light of your countenance, and we shall be whole.

The Collect of the day, or the following:

Give ear, O Lord, in this morning hour
to the prayers of your servants,
and in your mercy uncover and heal
the secret evil in our hearts,
that no dark desire may possess us
whom you have enlightened
with your heavenly grace;
through Jesus Christ our Lord.
Amen.

(Gelasian Sacramentary)

Silent prayer

Conclusion

The Lord be with you
and with your spirit.

Let us bless the Lord.
Thanks be to God.

May God in his great wisdom guide us throughout this day.
Amen.

MIDDAY PRAYER

Wednesday

O God, make speed to save us.
O Lord, make haste to help us.

**Glory to the Father, and to the Son,
and to the Holy Spirit;
as it was in the beginning, is now,
and shall be for ever. Amen.**

Hymn

**O God, who gives to humankind
a searching heart and questing mind:
grant us to find your truth and laws,
and wisdom to perceive their cause.**

**In all our learning give us grace
to bow ourselves before your face;
as knowledge grows, Lord, keep us free
from self-destructive vanity.**

**Sometimes we think we understand
all workings of your mighty hand;
then through your Son help us to know
those truths which you alone can show.**

**Teach us to joy in things revealed,
to search with care all yet concealed;
as through Christ's light your truth we find
and worship you with heart and mind.**

Psalm 65.4–13

Antiphon: **With wonders**

1 With wonders you will answer us in your righteousness,
    O God of our salvation,
  O hope of all the ends of the earth
    and of the farthest seas.

2 In your strength you set fast the mountains
  and are girded about with might.

3 You still the raging of the seas,
  the roaring of their waves
    and the clamour of the peoples.

4 Those who dwell at the ends of the earth
    tremble at your marvels;
  the gates of the morning and evening sing your praise.

5 You visit the earth and water it;
  you make it very plenteous.

6 The river of God is full of water;
  you prepare grain for your people,
    for so you provide for the earth.

7 You drench the furrows and smooth out the ridges;
  you soften the ground with showers and bless its
    increase.

8 You crown the year with your goodness,
  and your paths overflow with plenty.

9 May the pastures of the wilderness flow with goodness
  and the hills be girded with joy.

10 May the meadows be clothed with flocks of sheep
  and the valleys stand so thick with corn
    that they shall laugh and sing.

Glory to the Father, and to the Son,
and to the Holy Spirit;
as it was in the beginning, is now,
and shall be for ever. Amen.

Antiphon: **With wonders you will answer us in your righteousness**

Chapter
Matthew 11.28–30

Come to me, all you who are weary and burdened, and I will give you rest. Take my yoke upon you and learn from me, for I am gentle and humble in heart, and you will find rest for your souls. For my yoke is easy and my burden is light.

Thanks be to God.

Canticle
Philippians 2.5–11

Antiphon: **At the name of Jesus**

1 Your attitude should be
  the same as that of Christ Jesus:

2 Who being in very nature God,
  did not consider equality with God
    something to be grasped,

3 But made himself nothing,
  taking the very nature of a servant,
    being made in human likeness.

4 And being found in appearance as a man,
    he humbled himself
  and became obedient to death –
    even death on a cross!

5 Therefore God exalted him to the highest place
  and gave him the name that is above every name,

6 That at the name of Jesus every knee should bow,
  in heaven and on earth and under the earth,

7 And every tongue confess that Jesus Christ is Lord,
  to the glory of God the Father.

Antiphon: **At the name of Jesus every knee should bow**

The Prayers

The Kyries

Lord, have mercy.
Christ, have mercy.
Lord, have mercy.

The Lord's Prayer

**Our Father in heaven,
hallowed be your name,
your kingdom come,
your will be done,
on earth as in heaven.
Give us today our daily bread.
Forgive us our sins
as we forgive those who sin against us.
Lead us not into temptation
but deliver us from evil.
[For the kingdom, the power,
and the glory are yours
now and for ever.] Amen.**

O Lord, your word endures for ever in heaven.
Your truth also remains from one generation to another.

You are my shepherd;
therefore can I lack nothing.

You make me lie down in green pastures
and lead me beside still waters.

Your praise will always be in my mouth.
I will always give you thanks.

The Collect of the day, or the following:

May the grace of the Lord Jesus Christ
sanctify us and keep us from all evil;
may he drive far from us all hurtful things,
and purify both our souls and bodies;
may he bind us to himself by the bond of love,
and may his peace abound in our hearts.
Amen.

(*Gregorian Sacramentary*)

Conclusion

O Lord, hear our prayer
and let our cry come to you.

Let us bless the Lord.
Thanks be to God.

May God prosper the works of our hands
and bring us to his eternal kingdom.
Amen.

EVENING PRAYER

Wednesday

O Lord, open our lips
and our mouth shall proclaim your praise.

Let us worship the Lord.
All praise to his name.

Glory to the Father, and to the Son,
and to the Holy Spirit;
as it was in the beginning, is now,
and shall be for ever. Amen.

Evening hymn

Round me falls the night –
Saviour, be my light:
through the hours in darkness shrouded
let me see your face unclouded;
let your glory shine
in this heart of mine.

When my work is done
and my rest begun,
peaceful sleep and silence seeking
let me hear you softly speaking;
to my inward ear
whisper 'I am near.'

Holy, heavenly Light,
shining through earth's night,
joy and life and inspiration,
love enfolding every nation:
be with me tonight,
Saviour, be my light.

Psalm 65.1–7

Antiphon: **Happy are they**

1 Praise is due to you, O God, in Zion;
  to you that answer prayer shall vows be paid.

2 To you shall all flesh come to confess their sins;
    when our misdeeds prevail against us,
      you will purge them away.

3 Happy are they whom you choose
      and draw to your courts to dwell there.
  We shall be satisfied with the blessings of your house,
      even of your holy temple.

4 With wonders you will answer us in your righteousness,
      O God of our salvation,
  O hope of all the ends of the earth
      and of the farthest seas.

5 In your strength you set fast the mountains
      and are girded about with might.

6 You still the raging of the seas,
    the roaring of their waves
      and the clamour of the peoples.

7 Those who dwell at the ends of the earth
      tremble at your marvels;
  the gates of the morning and evening sing your praise.

Glory to the Father, and to the Son,
and to the Holy Spirit;
as it was in the beginning, is now,
and shall be for ever. Amen.

Antiphon: **Happy are they whom you choose**

Chapter
Mark 8.27–29

Jesus and his disciples went on to the villages around Caesarea Philippi. On the way he asked them, 'Who do people say I am?' They replied, 'Some say John the Baptist; others say Elijah; and still others, one of the prophets.' 'But what about you?' he asked. 'Who do you say I am?' Peter answered, 'You are the Christ.'

Thanks be to God.

O. T. reading

Magnificat – The Song of Mary
Luke 1.46–55

Antiphon: **He has mercy on those who fear him**

1 My soul proclaims the greatness of the Lord;
  my spirit rejoices in God my Saviour.

2 For he has looked with favour on his lowly servant;
  from this day all generations will call me blessed.

3 The Almighty has done great things for me,
  and holy is his name.

4 He has mercy on those who fear him
  in every generation.

5 He has shown the strength of his arm;
  he has scattered the proud in their conceit.

6 He has cast down the mighty from their thrones
  and has lifted up the lowly.

7 He has filled the hungry with good things
  and the rich he has sent away empty.

8 He has come to the help of his servant, Israel,
  for he has remembered his promise of mercy.

9 The promise he made to our forebears,
  to Abraham and his children for ever.

Glory to the Father, and to the Son,
and to the Holy Spirit;
as it was in the beginning, is now,
and shall be for ever. Amen.

Antiphon: **He has mercy on those who fear him in every generation**

N. T. reading

The Prayers

Happy are those you choose
and draw to your courts to dwell there.

The Kyries

Lord, have mercy.
Christ, have mercy.
Lord, have mercy.

The Lord's Prayer

Our Father in heaven,
hallowed be your name,
your kingdom come,
your will be done,
on earth as in heaven.
Give us today our daily bread.
Forgive us our sins
as we forgive those who sin against us.
Lead us not into temptation
but deliver us from evil.
[For the kingdom, the power,
and the glory are yours
now and for ever.] Amen.

I call to you with my whole heart.
Answer me, O Lord, that I may keep your statutes.

Early in the morning I cry to you,
for in your word is my trust.

My eyes are open before the night watches,
that I may meditate on your word.

Hear my voice, O Lord, according to your faithful love.
According to your judgement, give me life.

The Collect of the day, or the following:

O God, who fills the heavens and the earth,
ever active, ever at rest, you are everywhere
and everywhere are wholly present.
Who is not absent even when far off,
who with your whole being fills yet transcends all things,
who teaches the hearts of the faithful without the sound of
    words;
teach us, we pray,
through Jesus Christ our Lord.
Amen.

(St Augustine)

Silent prayer

Conclusion

The grace of our Lord Jesus Christ,
and the love of God,
and the fellowship of the Holy Spirit,
be with us all evermore.
Amen.

Let us bless the Lord.
Thanks be to God.

AN ORDER FOR COMPLINE
(A Late Evening Service)

Wednesday

The Lord Almighty grant us a quiet night and a perfect end.
Amen.

Be self-controlled and alert. Your enemy the devil prowls
around like a roaring lion looking for someone to devour.
Resist him, standing firm in the faith.

(1 Peter 5.8–9)

But you, O Lord, have mercy upon us.
Thanks be to God.

O God, make speed to save us.
O Lord, make haste to help us.

**Glory to the Father, and to the Son,
and to the Holy Spirit;
as it was in the beginning, is now,
and shall be for ever. Amen.**

Praise to the Lord.
The Lord's name be praised.

Psalm 91

1 Whoever dwells in the shelter of the Most High
   and abides under the shadow of the Almighty,

2 Shall say to the Lord, 'My refuge and my stronghold,
   my God, in whom I put my trust.'

3 For he shall deliver you from the snare of the fowler
   and from the deadly pestilence.

4 He shall cover you with his wings
      and you shall be safe under his feathers;
   his faithfulness shall be your shield and buckler.

5 You shall not be afraid of any terror by night,
   nor of the arrow that flies by day;

6 Of the pestilence that stalks in darkness,
   nor of the sickness that destroys at noonday.

7 Though a thousand fall at your side
      and ten thousand at your right hand,
   yet it shall not come near you.

8 Your eyes have only to behold
   to see the reward of the wicked.

9 Because you have made the Lord your refuge
   and the Most High your stronghold,

10 There shall no evil happen to you,
   neither shall any plague come near your tent.

11 For he shall give his angels charge over you,
   to keep you in all your ways.

12 They shall bear you in their hands,
   lest you dash your foot against a stone.

13 You shall tread upon the lion and adder;
   the young lion and the serpent you shall trample
      underfoot.

14 Because they have set their love upon me,
      therefore will I deliver them;
   I will lift them up, because they know my name.

15 They will call upon me and I will answer them;
   I am with them in trouble,
      I will deliver them and bring them to honour.

16 With long life will I satisfy them
   and show them my salvation.

Short lesson

I pray that out of his glorious riches he may strengthen you
with power through his Spirit in your inner being, so that
Christ may dwell in your hearts through faith. And I pray
that you, being rooted and established in love, may have
power, together with all the saints, to grasp how wide and
long and high and deep is the love of Christ, and to know
this love that surpasses knowledge – that you may be filled to
the measure of all the fullness of God.

(Ephesians 3.16–19)

Hymn

Saviour, again to your dear name we raise
with one accord our parting hymn of praise;
we give you thanks before our worship cease –
then, in the silence, hear your word of peace.

Give us your peace, Lord, through the coming night,
turn all our darkness to your perfect light;
then, through our sleep, our hope and strength renew,
for dark and light are both alike to you.

Give us your peace throughout our earthly life,
comfort in sorrow, courage in the strife;
then, when your voice shall make our conflict cease,
call us, O Lord, to your eternal peace.

Antiphon: Preserve us, O Lord, while waking, and guard us
while sleeping, that awake we may watch with Christ, and
asleep we may rest in peace.

The Prayers

The Kyries

Lord, have mercy.
Christ, have mercy.
Lord, have mercy.

The Lord's Prayer

Our Father in heaven,
hallowed be your name,
your kingdom come,
your will be done,
on earth as in heaven.
Give us today our daily bread.
Forgive us our sins
as we forgive those who sin against us.
Lead us not into temptation
but deliver us from evil.
[For the kingdom, the power,
and the glory are yours
now and for ever.] Amen.

I will bless the Lord who has given me counsel,
and in the night watches he instructs my heart.

I have set the Lord always before me.
He is at my right hand; I shall not fall.

Weigh my heart, examine me by night.
Refine me, and you will find no impurity in me.

We confess to God Almighty,
the Father, the Son, and the Holy Spirit,
that we have sinned in thought, word, and deed,
through our own grievous fault.
Therefore we pray God to have mercy upon us.

Almighty God, have mercy upon us,
forgive us, all our sins and deliver us from all evil,
confirm and strengthen us in all goodness,
and bring us to life everlasting;
through Jesus Christ our Lord.
Amen.

Will you not give us life again, O Lord:
that your people may rejoice in you?

Show us your mercy, O Lord,
and grant us your salvation.

Keep us tonight, Lord, from all sin.
Have mercy on us, Lord, have mercy.

Lord, hear our prayer
and let our cry come to you.

Collect

O Lord Jesus Christ, Son of the living God,
who at this evening hour rested in the sepulchre,
and did thereby sanctify the grave
to be a bed of hope to your people:
make us so to abound
in sorrow for our sins,
which were the cause of your Passion,
that when our bodies
lie in the dust,
our souls may live with you;
who lives and reigns with the Father and the Holy Spirit,
one God, world without end.
Amen.

Nunc Dimittis

1 Now, Lord, you let your servant go in peace:
   your word has been fulfilled.

2 My own eyes have seen the salvation
   which you have prepared in the sight of every people:

3 A light to reveal you to the nations
   and the glory of your people Israel.

Glory to the Father, and to the Son,
and to the Holy Spirit;
as it was in the beginning, is now,
and shall be for ever. Amen.

We will lay us down in peace and take our rest,
for it is you, Lord, only who make us dwell in safety.

The Lord be with you
and with your spirit.

Let us bless the Lord.
Thanks be to God.

The Almighty and merciful Lord,
the Father, the Son, and the Holy Spirit,
bless and preserve us. Amen.

Thursday

MORNING PRAYER

Thursday

In the name of the Father, and of the Son, and of the
  Holy Spirit.
Amen.

I will bless the Lord at all times.
His praise shall ever be in my mouth.

My soul shall glory in the Lord.
Let the humble hear and be glad.

**Glory to the Father, and to the Son,
and to the Holy Spirit;
as it was in the beginning, is now,
and shall be for ever. Amen.**

Morning hymn

**Give praise to God, who safely kept
and well refreshed me while I slept:
grant, Lord, that when from death I wake
I may of endless life partake.**

**To you my vows I here renew:
disperse my sins as morning dew;
guard my first springs of thought and will,
and with your love my spirit fill.**

**Direct, control, suggest this day
all I desire or do or say;
that all my powers with all their might
for your sole glory may unite.**

**Praise God, from whom all blessings flow
in heaven above and earth below;
one God, three persons, we adore
to him be praise for evermore!**

Psalm 34.11–22

Antiphon: **The eyes of the Lord**

1 Come, my children, and listen to me;
   I will teach you the fear of the Lord.

2 Who is there who delights in life
   and longs for days to enjoy good things?

3 Keep your tongue from evil
   and your lips from lying words.

4 Turn from evil and do good;
   seek peace and pursue it.

5 The eyes of the Lord are upon the righteous
   and his ears are open to their cry.

6 The face of the Lord is against those who do evil,
   to root out the remembrance of them from the earth.

7 The righteous cry and the Lord hears them
   and delivers them out of all their troubles.

8 The Lord is near to the brokenhearted
   and will save those who are crushed in spirit.

9 Many are the troubles of the righteous;
   from them all will the Lord deliver them.

10 He keeps all their bones,
   so that not one of them is broken.

11 But evil shall slay the wicked
   and those who hate the righteous will be condemned.

12 The Lord ransoms the life of his servants
   and will condemn none who seek refuge in him.

Glory to the Father, and to the Son,
and to the Holy Spirit;
as it was in the beginning, is now,
and shall be for ever. Amen.

Antiphon: **The eyes of the Lord are upon the righteous**

Chapter
Matthew 5.14–15

You are the light of the world. A city on a hill cannot be hidden. Neither do people light a lamp and put it under a bowl. Instead they put it on its stand, and it gives light to everyone in the house.

Thanks be to God.

Lectionary readings – if you have time, one or both

O. T. reading

Psalm 119.129–136

1 Your testimonies are wonderful;
   therefore my soul keeps them.

2 The opening of your word gives light;
   it gives understanding to the simple.

3 I open my mouth and draw in my breath,
   as I long for your commandments.

4 Turn to me and be gracious to me,
   as is your way with those who love your name.

5 Order my steps by your word,
   and let no wickedness have dominion over me.

6 Redeem me from earthly oppressors
   so that I may keep your commandments.

7 Show the light of your countenance upon your servant
   and teach me your statutes.

8 My eyes run down with streams of water,
   because the wicked do not keep your law.

**Glory to the Father, and to the Son,
and to the Holy Spirit;
as it was in the beginning, is now,
and shall be for ever. Amen.**

N. T. reading

Canticle
Revelation 4.11, 5.9b–10

Antiphon: **You are worthy**

1 'You are worthy, our Lord and God,
    to receive glory and honour and power,
  for you created all things,
    and by your will they were created and have their
      being.'

2 'You are worthy to take the scroll
    and to open its seals, because you were slain,
  and with your blood you purchased men for God
    from every tribe and language and people and nation.

3 You have made them to be a kingdom
    and priests to serve our God,
  and they will reign on the earth.'

Glory to the Father, and to the Son,
and to the Holy Spirit;
as it was in the beginning, is now,
and shall be for ever. Amen.

Antiphon: **You are worthy, our Lord and God**

The Prayers

The Kyries

Lord, have mercy.
Christ, have mercy.
Lord, have mercy.

The Lord's Prayer

Our Father in heaven,
hallowed be your name,
your kingdom come,
your will be done,
on earth as in heaven.
Give us today our daily bread.
Forgive us our sins
as we forgive those who sin against us.
Lead us not into temptation
but deliver us from evil.
[For the kingdom, the power,
and the glory are yours
now and for ever.] Amen.

I will bless the Lord at all times.
His praise shall ever be in my mouth.

O magnify the Lord with me.
Let us exalt his name together.

The Collect of the day, or the following:

Lord God Almighty,
open my heart and enlighten me
by the grace of your Holy Spirit,
that I may seek what is pleasing to your will;
direct my thoughts and desires
to think and do those things that will make me
able to attain your everlasting joys in heaven;
order my ways in your commandments
that I may be dilligent to fulfil them
and receive the eternal reward.
Amen.

(*The venerable Bede*)

Silent prayer

Conclusion

The Lord be with you
and with your spirit.

Let us bless the Lord
Thanks be to God.

The Lord bless us and watch over us during this day,
and guide us into that inner peace of the kingdom of God.
Amen.

MIDDAY PRAYER

Thursday

O God, make speed to save us.
O Lord, make haste to help us.

**Glory to the Father, and to the Son,
and to the Holy Spirit;
as it was in the beginning, is now,
and shall be for ever. Amen.**

Hymn

**O dearest Lord, thy sacred head
with thorns was pierced for me;
O pour thy blessing on my head
that I may think for thee.**

**O dearest Lord, thy sacred hands
with nails were pierced for me;
O shed thy blessing on my hands
that they may work for thee.**

**O dearest Lord, thy sacred feet
with nails were pierced for me;
O pour thy blessing on my feet
that they may follow thee.**

**O dearest Lord, thy sacred heart
with spear was pierced for me;
O pour thy Spirit in my heart
that I may live for thee.**

Psalm 23

1 The Lord is my shepherd;
   therefore can I lack nothing.

2 He makes me lie down in green pastures
   and leads me beside still waters.

3 He shall refresh my soul
   and guide me in the paths of righteousness for his name's
       sake.

4 Though I walk through the valley of the shadow of death,
       I will fear no evil;
   for you are with me;
       your rod and your staff, they comfort me.

5 You spread a table before me
       in the presence of those who trouble me;
   you have anointed my head with oil
       and my cup shall be full.

6 Surely goodness and loving mercy shall follow me
       all the days of my life,
   and I will dwell in the house of the Lord for ever.

Glory to the Father, and to the Son,
and to the Holy Spirit;
as it was in the beginning, is now,
and shall be for ever. Amen.

Antiphon: **He shall refresh my soul and guide me**

Chapter
Revelation 22.12–14

Behold, I am coming soon! My reward is with me, and I will give to everyone according to what he has done. I am the Alpha and the Omega, the First and the Last, the Beginning and the End. Blessed are those who wash their robes, that they may have the right to the tree of life and may go through the gates into the city.

Thanks be to God.

Canticle
Revelation 5.12b–13

Antiphon: **In a loud voice**

1 'Worthy is the Lamb, who was slain,
     to receive power and wealth and wisdom and strength
   and honour and glory and praise!'

2 Then I heard every creature in heaven and on earth
     and under the earth and on the sea,
     and all that is in them, singing:
  'To him who sits on the throne and to the Lamb
     be praise and honour and glory and power,
     for ever and ever!'

Antiphon: **In a loud voice they sang**

The Prayers

The Kyries

Lord, have mercy.
Christ, have mercy.
Lord, have mercy.

The Lord's Prayer

Our Father in heaven,
hallowed be your name,
your kingdom come,
your will be done,
on earth as in heaven.
Give us today our daily bread.
Forgive us our sins
as we forgive those who sin against us.
Lead us not into temptation
but deliver us from evil.
[For the kingdom, the power,
and the glory are yours
now and for ever.] Amen.

O Lord, arise, help us
and deliver us for your name's sake.

Your love, O Lord, reaches to the heavens
and your faithfulness to the clouds.

Your righteousness stands like the strong mountains,
your justice like the great deep.

How precious is your loving mercy, O God!
All mortal flesh shall take refuge under the shadow of your
wings.

The Collect of the day, or the following:

O God,
who resists the proud, and gives grace to the humble;
give us the virtue of true humility,
of which your only Son
himself gave us the perfect example;
that we may never offend you by our pride,
and be rejected for our self-assertion;
through Jesus Christ our Lord.
Amen.

Conclusion

O Lord, hear our prayer
and let our cry come to you.

Let us bless the Lord.
Thanks be to God.

May God guard and bless all those we love and work with.
Amen.

EVENING PRAYER

Thursday

O Lord, open our lips
and our mouth shall proclaim your praise.

Come to us in your greatness
and make your home within us.

Glory to the Father, and to the Son,
and to the Holy Spirit;
as it was in the beginning, is now,
and shall be for ever. Amen.

Evening hymn

O Trinity, most blessed light,
O Unity of sovereign might,
as now the fiery sun departs
shed thou thy beams within our hearts.

To thee our morning song of praise,
to thee our evening prayer we raise;
thee may our souls for evermore
in lowly reverence adore.

All praise to God the Father be,
all praise, eternal Son, to thee,
whom with the Spirit we adore,
for ever and evermore.
Amen.

Psalm 138

Antiphon: **In the day that I called**

1 I will give thanks to you, O Lord, with my whole heart;
   before the gods will I sing praise to you.

2 I will bow down towards your holy temple and praise your
         name,
      because of your love and faithfulness;
   for you have glorified your name
      and your word above all things.

3 In the day that I called to you, you answered me;
   you put new strength in my soul.

4 All the kings of the earth shall praise you, O Lord,
   for they have heard the words of your mouth.

5 They shall sing of the ways of the Lord,
   that great is the glory of the Lord.

6 Though the Lord be high, he watches over the lowly;
   as for the proud, he regards them from afar.

7 Though I walk in the midst of trouble, you will preserve
         me;
      you will stretch forth your hand against the fury of my
         enemies;
      your right hand will save me.

8 The Lord shall make good his purpose for me;
   your loving-kindness, O Lord, endures for ever;
      forsake not the work of your hands.

Glory to the Father, and to the Son,
and to the Holy Spirit;
as it was in the beginning, is now,
and shall be for ever. Amen.

Antiphon: **In the day that I called to you, you answered me**

Chapter
Luke 10.23–24

Then he turned to his disciples and said privately, 'Blessed are the eyes that see what you see. For I tell you that many prophets and kings wanted to see what you see but did not see it, and to hear what you hear but did not hear it.'

Thanks be to God.

Lectionary readings – if you have time, one or both

O. T. reading

Magnificat – The Song of Mary
Luke 1.46–55

Antiphon: **For he has looked with favour**

1 My soul proclaims the greatness of the Lord;
  my spirit rejoices in God my Saviour.

2 For he has looked with favour on his lowly servant;
  from this day all generations will call me blessed.

3 The Almighty has done great things for me,
  and holy is his name.

4 He has mercy on those who fear him
  in every generation.

5 He has shown the strength of his arm;
  he has scattered the proud in their conceit.

6 He has cast down the mighty from their thrones
  and has lifted up the lowly.

7 He has filled the hungry with good things
  and the rich he has sent away empty.

8 He has come to the help of his servant, Israel,
  for he has remembered his promise of mercy.

9 The promise he made to our forebears,
  to Abraham and his children for ever.

Glory to the Father, and to the Son,
and to the Holy Spirit;
as it was in the beginning, is now,
and shall be for ever. Amen.

Antiphon: **For he has looked with favour on his lowly servant**

N. T. reading

The Prayers

Let the heavens rejoice
and let the earth be glad.

The Kyries

Lord, have mercy.
Christ, have mercy.
Lord, have mercy.

The Lord's Prayer

Our Father in heaven,
hallowed be your name,
your kingdom come,
your will be done,
on earth as in heaven.
Give us today our daily bread.
Forgive us our sins
as we forgive those who sin against us.
Lead us not into temptation
but deliver us from evil.
[For the kingdom, the power,
and the glory are yours
now and for ever.] Amen.

Let the heavens rejoice and let the earth be glad.
Let the sea thunder and all that is in it.

Let the fields be joyful and all that is in them.
Let all the trees of the wood shout for joy before the Lord.

For he comes, he comes to judge the earth with
righteousness.
He will judge the world and the peoples with his truth.

The Collect of the day, or the following:

God be in my head, and in my understanding;
God be in my eyes, and in my looking;
God be in my mouth, and in my speaking;
God be in my heart, and in my thinking;
God be at my end, and at my departing.
Amen.

(Sarum primer)

Silent prayer

Conclusion

O Lord, hear our prayer
and let our cry come to you.

Let us bless the Lord.
Thanks be to God.

God keep us safe in our journeying to and from home and those we love.
Amen.

AN ORDER FOR COMPLINE
(A Late Evening Service)

Thursday

The Lord Almighty grant us a quiet night and a perfect end.
Amen.

Be self-controlled and alert. Your enemy the devil prowls
around like a roaring lion looking for someone to devour.
Resist him, standing firm in the faith.

(1 Peter 5.8–9)

But you, O Lord, have mercy upon us.
Thanks be to God.

O God, make speed to save us.
O Lord, make haste to help us.

**Glory to the Father, and to the Son,
and to the Holy Spirit;
as it was in the beginning, is now,
and shall be for ever. Amen.**

Praise to the Lord.
The Lord's name be praised.

Psalm 13

1 How long will you forget me, O Lord; for ever?
  How long will you hide your face from me?

2 How long shall I have anguish in my soul
    and grief in my heart, day after day?
  How long shall my enemy triumph over me?

3 Look upon me and answer, O Lord my God;
  lighten my eyes, lest I sleep in death;

4 Lest my enemy say, 'I have prevailed against him,'
  and my foes rejoice that I have fallen.

5 But I put my trust in your steadfast love;
  my heart will rejoice in your salvation.

6 I will sing to the Lord,
  for he has dealt so bountifully with me.

Short lesson

Therefore watch, because you do not know on what day
your Lord will come. But understand this: If the owner of
the house had known at what time of night the thief was
coming, he would have kept watch and would not have let
his house be broken into. So you also must be ready, because
the Son of Man will come at an hour when you do not
expect him.

(Matthew 24.42–44)

Hymn

Before the ending of the day,
Creator of the world we pray,
that with thy wonted favour thou
wouldst be our guard and keeper now.

From all ill dreams defend our eyes,
from nightly fears and fantasies;
tread under foot our ghostly foe,
that no pollution we may know.

O Father, that we ask be done,
through Jesus Christ, thine only Son;
who, with the Holy Ghost and thee,
doth live and reign eternally.

Antiphon: Preserve us, O Lord, while waking, and guard us
while sleeping, that awake we may watch with Christ, and
asleep we may rest in peace.

The Prayers

The Kyries

Lord, have mercy.
Christ, have mercy.
Lord, have mercy.

The Lord's Prayer

Our Father in heaven,
hallowed be your name,
your kingdom come,
your will be done,
on earth as in heaven.
Give us today our daily bread.
Forgive us our sins
as we forgive those who sin against us.
Lead us not into temptation
but deliver us from evil.
[For the kingdom, the power,
and the glory are yours
now and for ever.] Amen.

I will bless the Lord who has given me counsel,
and in the night watches he instructs my heart.

I have set the Lord always before me.
He is at my right hand; I shall not fall.

Weigh my heart, examine me by night.
Refine me, and you will find no impurity in me.

We confess to God Almighty,
the Father, the Son, and the Holy Spirit,
that we have sinned in thought, word, and deed,
through our own grievous fault.
Therefore we pray God to have mercy upon us.

Almighty God, have mercy upon us,
forgive us all our sins and deliver us from all evil,
confirm and strengthen us in all goodness,
and bring us to life everlasting;
through Jesus Christ our Lord.
Amen.

Will you not give us life again, O Lord:
that your people may rejoice in you?

Show us your mercy, O Lord,
and grant us your salvation.

Keep us tonight, Lord, from all sin.
Have mercy on us, Lord, have mercy.

Lord, hear our prayer
and let our cry come to you.

Collect

Look down, O Lord, from your heavenly throne,
illuminate the darkness of this night with your celestial
    brightness,
and from the sons of light banish the deeds of darkness;
through Jesus Christ our Lord.
Amen.

Nunc Dimittis

1 Now, Lord, you let your servant go in peace:
   your word has been fulfilled.

2 My own eyes have seen the salvation
   which you have prepared in the sight of every people:

3 A light to reveal you to the nations
   and the glory of your people Israel.

Glory to the Father, and to the Son,
and to the Holy Spirit;
as it was in the beginning, is now,
and shall be for ever. Amen.

We will lay us down in peace and take our rest,
for it is you, Lord, only who make us dwell in safety.

The Lord be with you
and with your spirit.

Let us bless the Lord.
Thanks be to God.

**The Almighty and merciful Lord,
the Father, the Son, and the Holy Spirit,
bless and preserve us. Amen.**

Friday

MORNING PRAYER

Friday

In the name of the Father, and of the Son, and of the
Holy Spirit.
Amen.

O Lord, open our lips
and our mouths shall proclaim your praise.

O God, make speed to save us.
O Lord, make haste to help us.

**Glory to the Father, and to the Son,
and to the Holy Spirit;
as it was in the beginning, is now,
and shall be for ever. Amen.**

Morning hymn

**Morning has broken like the first morning,
blackbird has spoken like the first bird.
Praise for the singing!
Praise for the morning!
Praise for them, springing
fresh from the Word!**

**Sweet the rain's new fall, sunlit from heaven,
like the first dewfall on the first grass.
Praise for the sweetness of the wet garden,
sprung in completeness where his feet pass.**

**Mine is the sunlight! Mine is the morning,
born of the one light Eden saw play!
Praise with elation, praise ev'ry morning,
God's recreation of the new day!**

Psalm 108.1–6

1 My heart is ready, O God, my heart is ready;
  I will sing and give you praise.

2 Awake, my soul; awake, harp and lyre,
  that I may awaken the dawn.

3 I will give you thanks, O Lord, among the peoples;
  I will sing praise to you among the nations.

4 For your loving-kindness is as high as the heavens
  and your faithfulness reaches to the clouds.

5 Be exalted, O God, above the heavens
  and your glory over all the earth.

6 That your beloved may be delivered,
  save us by your right hand and answer me.

Glory to the Father, and to the Son,
and to the Holy Spirit;
as it was in the beginning, is now,
and shall be for ever. Amen.

Antiphon: **Be exalted, O God, above the heavens**

Chapter
Matthew 5.43–45

You have heard that it was said, 'Love your neighbour and
hate your enemy.' But I tell you: Love your enemies and pray
for those who persecute you, that you may be sons of your
Father in heaven. He causes his sun to rise on the evil and the
good, and sends rain on the righteous and the unrighteous.

Thanks be to God.

Lectionary readings – if you have time, one or both

O. T. reading

Psalm 1.1–3

1 Blessed are they who have not walked
    in the counsel of the wicked,
  nor lingered in the way of sinners,
    nor sat in the assembly of the scornful.

2 Their delight is in the law of the Lord
  and they meditate on his law day and night.

3 Like a tree planted by streams of water
    bearing fruit in due season, with leaves that do not
      wither,
  whatever they do, it shall prosper.

**Glory to the Father, and to the Son,
and to the Holy Spirit;
as it was in the beginning, is now,
and shall be for ever. Amen.**

N. T. reading

Canticle

The Song of the Three 29–34

Antiphon: **Blessed are you**

1 Blessed are you, the God of our ancestors,
  worthy to be praised and exalted for ever.

2 Blessed is your holy and glorious name,
  worthy to be praised and exalted for ever.

3 Blessed are you, in your holy and glorious temple,
  worthy to be praised and exalted for ever.

4 Blessed are you who look into the depths,
  worthy to be praised and exalted for ever.

5 Blessed are you, enthroned on the cherubim,
  worthy to be praised and exalted for ever.

6 Blessed are you on the throne of your kingdom,
  worthy to be praised and exalted for ever.

7 Blessed are you in the heights of heaven,
  worthy to be praised and exalted for ever.

Glory to the Father, and to the Son,
and to the Holy Spirit;
as it was in the beginning, is now,
and shall be for ever. Amen.

Antiphon: **Blessed are you, on the throne of your kingdom**

The Prayers

The Kyries

Lord, have mercy.
Christ, have mercy.
Lord, have mercy.

The Lord's Prayer

Our Father in heaven,
hallowed be your name,
your kingdom come,
your will be done,
on earth as in heaven.
Give us today our daily bread.
Forgive us our sins
as we forgive those who sin against us.
Lead us not into temptation
but deliver us from evil.
[For the kingdom, the power,
and the glory are yours
now and for ever.] Amen.

Save your people, Lord, and bless your inheritance.
Govern and uphold them now and always.

Day by day we bless you.
We praise your name for ever.

Keep us today, Lord, from all sin.
Have mercy on us, Lord, have mercy.

The Collect of the day, or the following:

Almighty God,
for as much as without you we
are not able to please you;
mercifully grant that your
Holy Spririt may in all things
direct and rule our hearts;
through Jesus Christ our Lord.
Amen.

Silent prayer

Conclusion

The Lord be with you
and with your spirit.

Let us bless the Lord.
Thanks be to God.

May the light of Christ shine through us this day
in all that we say and do and think.
Amen.

MIDDAY PRAYER

Friday

O God, make speed to save us.
O Lord, make haste to help us.

**Glory to the Father, and to the Son,
and to the Holy Spirit;
as it was in the beginning, is now,
and shall be for ever. Amen.**

Hymn

**Be thou my guardian and my guide,
and hear me when I call;
let not my slipp'ry footsteps slide,
and hold me lest I fall.**

**The world, the flesh, and Satan dwell
around the path I tread;
O save me from the snares of hell,
thou quick'ner of the dead.**

**And if I tempted am to sin,
and outward things are strong,
do thou, O Lord, keep watch within,
and save my soul from wrong.**

**Still let me ever watch and pray,
and feel that I am frail;
that if the tempter cross my way,
yet he may not prevail.**

Psalm 37.1–9

Antiphon: **Trust in the Lord**

1 Fret not because of evildoers;
  be not jealous of those who do wrong.

2 For they shall soon wither like grass
  and like the green herb fade away.

3 Trust in the Lord and be doing good;
  dwell in the land and be nourished with truth.

4 Let your delight be in the Lord
  and he will give you your heart's desire.

5 Commit your way to the Lord and put your trust in him,
  and he will bring it to pass.

6 He will make your righteousness as clear as the light
  and your just dealing as the noonday.

7 Be still before the Lord and wait for him;
  do not fret over those that prosper
    as they follow their evil schemes.

8 Refrain from anger and abandon wrath;
  do not fret, lest you be moved to do evil.

9 For evildoers shall be cut off,
  but those who wait upon the Lord
    shall possess the land.

Glory to the Father, and to the Son,
and to the Holy Spirit;
as it was in the beginning, is now,
and shall be for ever. Amen.

Antiphon: **Trust in the Lord and be doing good**

Work and Prayer

Chapter

1 John 4.16b–18

God is love. Whoever lives in love lives in God, and God in
him. In this way, love is made complete among us so that we
will have confidence on the day of judgement, because in
this world we are like him. There is no fear in love. But
perfect love drives out fear, because fear has to do with
punishment. The one who fears is not made perfect in love.

Thanks be to God.

Canticle

Romans 11.33–36

Antiphon: **Let us rejoice**

1 Oh, the depth of the riches of the wisdom and knowledge
    of God!
   How unsearchable his judgements, and his paths beyond
        tracing out!

2 'Who has known the mind of the Lord?
   Or who has been his counsellor?'

3 'Who has ever given to God,
   that God should repay him?'

4 For from him and through him and to him are all things.
   To him be the glory for ever! Amen.

Antiphon: **Let us rejoice and be glad**

The Prayers

The Kyries

Lord, have mercy.
Christ, have mercy.
Lord, have mercy.

The Lord's Prayer

Our Father in heaven,
hallowed be your name,
your kingdom come,
your will be done,
on earth as in heaven.
Give us today our daily bread.
Forgive us our sins
as we forgive those who sin against us.
Lead us not into temptation
but deliver us from evil.
[For the kingdom, the power,
and the glory are yours
now and for ever.] Amen.

I will bless the Lord at all times.
His praise shall ever be in my mouth.

My soul shall glory in the Lord.
Let the humble hear and be glad.

O magnify the Lord with me.
Let us exalt his name together.

I sought the Lord and he answered me
and delivered me from all my fears.

Look upon him and be radiant
and your faces shall not be ashamed.

The Collect of the Day, or the following:

Grant, O Lord, that in your wounds we may find our safety.
In your stripes our healing,
in your pain our peace,
in your cross our victory,
in your resurrection our triumph,
and a crown of righteousness
in your eternal kingdom.
Amen.

(Jeremy Taylor)

Conclusion

O Lord, hear our prayer
and let our cry come to you.

Let us bless the Lord.
Thanks be to God.

May God give us the grace of humility in all we do.
Amen.

EVENING PRAYER

Friday

O Lord, open our lips
and our mouth shall proclaim your praise.

The Lord is the strength of his people,
a safe refuge for his anointed.

**Glory to the Father, and to the Son,
and to the Holy Spirit;
as it was in the beginning, is now,
and shall be for ever. Amen.**

Evening hymn

**God that madest earth and heaven,
darkness and light;
who the day for toil hast given,
for rest the night:
may thine angel-guards defend us,
slumber sweet thy mercy send us,
holy dreams and hopes attend us,
this live-long night.**

**Guard us waking, guard us sleeping,
and, when we die,
may we in thy mighty keeping
all peaceful lie:
when the last dread call shall wake us,
do not thou our God forsake us,
but to reign in glory take us
with thee on high.**

Psalm 29

1 Ascribe to the Lord, you powers of heaven,
   ascribe to the Lord glory and strength.

2 Ascribe to the Lord the honour due to his name;
   worship the Lord in the beauty of holiness.

3 The voice of the Lord is upon the waters;
     the God of glory thunders;
   the Lord is upon the mighty waters.

4 The voice of the Lord is mighty in operation;
   the voice of the Lord is a glorious voice.

5 The voice of the Lord breaks the cedar trees;
   the Lord breaks the cedars of Lebanon;

6 He makes Lebanon skip like a calf
   and Sirion like a young wild ox.

7 The voice of the Lord splits the flash of lightning;
     the voice of the Lord shakes the wilderness;
   the Lord shakes the wilderness of Kadesh.

8 The voice of the Lord makes the oak trees writhe
     and strips the forests bare;
   in his temple all cry, 'Glory!'

9 The Lord sits enthroned above the water flood;
   the Lord sits enthroned as king for evermore.

10 The Lord shall give strength to his people;
   the Lord shall give his people the blessing of peace.

Glory to the Father, and to the Son,
and to the Holy Spirit;
as it was in the beginning, is now,
and shall be for ever. Amen.

Chapter
Matthew 7.1–2

Do not judge, or you too will be judged. For in the same way as you judge others, you will be judged, and with the measure you use, it will be measured to you.

Thanks be to God.

Lectionary readings – *if you have time, one or both*

O. T. reading

Magnificat – The Song of Mary
Luke 1. 46–55

Antiphon: **For he has looked with favour**

1 My soul proclaims the greatness of the Lord;
   my spirit rejoices in God my Saviour.

2 For he has looked with favour on his lowly servant;
   from this day all generations will call me blessed.

3 The Almighty has done great things for me,
   and holy is his name.

4 He has mercy on those who fear him
   in every generation.

5 He has shown the strength of his arm;
   he has scattered the proud in their conceit.

6 He has cast down the mighty from their thrones
   and has lifted up the lowly.

7 He has filled the hungry with good things
   and the rich he has sent away empty.

8 He has come to the help of his servant, Israel,
   for he has remembered his promise of mercy.

9 The promise he made to our forebears,
   to Abraham and his children for ever.

Glory to the Father, and to the Son,
and to the Holy Spirit;
as it was in the beginning, is now,
and shall be for ever. Amen.

Antiphon: **For he has looked with favour on his lowly**
servant

N. T. reading

The Prayers

Blessed be the Lord,
for he has heard my prayer.

The Kyries

Lord, have mercy.
Christ, have mercy.
Lord, have mercy.

The Lord's Prayer

Our Father in heaven,
hallowed be your name,
your kingdom come,
your will be done,
on earth as in heaven.
Give us today our daily bread.
Forgive us our sins
as we forgive those who sin against us.
Lead us not into temptation
but deliver us from evil.
[For the kingdom, the power,
and the glory are yours
now and for ever.] Amen.

I said Lord be merciful to me.
Heal my soul because I have sinned against you.

Turn again, O Lord, at the last
and be gracious to your servants.

Let your merciful kindness be upon us,
for we put our trust in you.

Let your priests be clothed with righteousness
and your people sing with joyfulness.

O Lord, save our nation
and teach those who govern us wisdom.

The Collect of the day, or the following:

Almighty and everlasting God,
you have given us your servants grace,
by the confession of a true faith,
to acknowledge the glory of the eternal Trinity
and in the power of the divine majesty to worship the Unity:
keep us steadfast in this faith,
that we may evermore be defended from all adversities;
through Jesus Christ your Son our Lord,
who is alive and reigns with you,
in the unity of the Holy Spirit,
one God, now and for ever.
Amen.

Silent prayer

Conclusion

The Lord be with you
and with your spirit.

Let us bless the Lord.
Thanks be to God.

May God bless us and keep us
and make our homes images of his eternal kingdom.
Amen.

AN ORDER FOR COMPLINE
(A Late Evening Service)

Friday

The Lord Almighty grant us a quiet night and a perfect end.
Amen.

Be self-controlled and alert. Your enemy the devil prowls
around like a roaring lion looking for someone to devour.
Resist him, standing firm in the faith.

(1 Peter 5.8–9)

But you, O Lord, have mercy upon us.
Thanks be to God.

O God, make speed to save us.
O Lord, make haste to help us.

Glory to the Father, and to the Son,
and to the Holy Spirit;
as it was in the beginning, is now,
and shall be for ever. Amen

Praise to the Lord.
The Lord's name be praised.

Psalm 130

1 Out of the depths have I cried to you, O Lord;
    Lord, hear my voice;
  let your ears consider well the voice of my supplication.

2 If you, Lord, were to mark what is done amiss,
  O Lord, who could stand?

3 But there is forgiveness with you,
  so that you shall be feared.

4 I wait for the Lord; my soul waits for him;
  in his word is my hope.

5 My soul waits for the Lord,
    more than the night watch for the morning,
  more than the night watch for the morning.

6 O Israel, wait for the Lord,
  for with the Lord there is mercy;

7 With him is plenteous redemption
  and he shall redeem Israel from all their sins.

Short lesson

But I tell you who hear me: Love your enemies, do good to those who hate you, bless those who curse you, pray for those who ill-treat you. If someone strikes you on one cheek, turn to him the other also. If someone takes your cloak, do not stop him from taking your tunic. Give to everyone who asks you, and if anyone takes what belongs to you, do not demand it back. Do to others as you would have them do to you.

(Luke 6.27–31)

Hymn

Glory to you, my God, this night
for all the blessings of the light;
keep me, O keep me, King of kings,
beneath your own Almighty wings.

Forgive me, Lord, through your dear Son,
the wrong that I this day have done,
that peace with God and man may be,
before I sleep, restored to me.

Teach me to live, that I may dread
the grave as little as my bed;
teach me to die, that so I may
rise glorious at the awesome day.

O may my soul on you repose
and restful sleep my eyelids close;
sleep that shall me more vigorous make
to serve my God when I awake.

Antiphon: Preserve us, O Lord, while waking, and guard us
while sleeping, that awake we may watch with Christ, and
asleep we may rest in peace.

The Prayers

The Kyries

Lord, have mercy.
Christ, have mercy.
Lord, have mercy.

The Lord's Prayer

Our Father in heaven,
hallowed be your name,
your kingdom come,
your will be done,
on earth as in heaven.
Give us today our daily bread.
Forgive us our sins
as we forgive those who sin against us.
Lead us not into temptation
but deliver us from evil.
[For the kingdom, the power,
and the glory are yours
now and for ever.] Amen.

I will bless the Lord who has given me counsel,
and in the night watches he instructs my heart.

I have set the Lord always before me.
He is at my right hand; I shall not fall.

Weigh my heart, examine me by night.
Refine me, and you will find no impurity in me.

We confess to God Almighty,
the Father, the Son, and the Holy Spirit,
that we have sinned in thought, word, and deed,
through our own grievous fault.
Therefore we pray God to have mercy upon us.

Almighty God, have mercy upon us,
forgive us all our sins and deliver us from all evil,
confirm and strengthen us in all goodness,
and bring us to life everlasting;
through Jesus Christ our Lord.
Amen.

Will you not give us life again, O Lord:
that your people may rejoice in you?

Show us your mercy, O Lord,
and grant us your salvation.

Keep us tonight, Lord, from all sin.
Have mercy on us, Lord, have mercy.

Lord, hear our prayer
and let our cry come to you.

Collect

Be present, O merciful God,
and protect us through the silent hours of this night,
so that we who are wearied by the changes and chances of
    this fleeting world,
may repose upon your eternal changelessness;
through Jesus Christ our Lord.
Amen.

Nunc Dimittis

1 Now, Lord, you let your servant go in peace:
  your word has been fulfilled.

2 My own eyes have seen the salvation
  which you have prepared in the sight of every people:

3 A light to reveal you to the nations
  and the glory of your people Israel.

Glory to the Father, and to the Son,
and to the Holy Spirit;
as it was in the beginning, is now,
and shall be for ever. Amen.

We will lay us down in peace and take our rest,
for it is you, Lord, only who make us dwell in safety.

The Lord be with you
and with your spirit.

Let us bless the Lord.
Thanks be to God.

**The Almighty and merciful Lord,
the Father, the Son, and the Holy Spirit,
bless and preserve us. Amen.**

Saturday

MORNING PRAYER

Saturday

In the name of the Father, and of the Son, and of the
  Holy Spirit.
Amen.

O Lord, open our lips
and our mouths shall proclaim your praise.

O God, make speed to save us.
O Lord, make haste to help us.

Glory to the Father, and to the Son,
and to the Holy Spirit;
as it was in the beginning, is now,
and shall be for ever. Amen.

Morning hymn

Lord, as the day begins
lift up our hearts in praise;
take from us all our sins,
guard us in all our ways:
our every step direct and guide
that Christ in all be glorified!

Christ be in work and skill,
serving each other's need;
Christ be in thought and will,
Christ be in word and deed:
our minds be set on things above
in joy and peace, in faith and love.

Grant us the Spirit's strength,
teach us to walk his way;
so bring us all at length
safe to the close of day:
from hour to hour sustain and bless,
and let our song be thankfulness.

Now as the day begins
make it the best of days;
take from us all our sins,
guard us in all our ways:
our every step direct and guide
that Christ in all be glorified!

Psalm 100

Antiphon: **O be joyful**

1 O be joyful in the Lord, all the earth;
  serve the Lord with gladness
    and come before his presence with a song.

2 Know that the Lord is God;
  it is he that has made us and we are his;
    we are his people and the sheep of his pasture.

3 Enter his gates with thanksgiving
    and his courts with praise;
  give thanks to him and bless his name.

4 For the Lord is gracious; his steadfast love is everlasting,
  and his faithfulness endures from generation to
      generation.

Glory to the Father, and to the Son,
and to the Holy Spirit;
as it was in the beginning, is now,
and shall be for ever. Amen.

Antiphon: **O be joyful in the Lord, all the earth**

Chapter
Matthew 6.25–27

Therefore I tell you, do not worry about your life, what you
will eat or drink; or about your body, what you will wear. Is
not life more important than food, and the body more
important than clothes? Look at the birds of the air; they do
not sow or reap or store away in barns, and yet your
heavenly Father feeds them. Are you not much more
valuable than they? Who of you by worrying can add a
single hour to his life?

Lectionary readings – if you have time, one or both

O.T. reading

Psalm 145.9–14

1 The Lord is loving to everyone
and his mercy is over all his creatures.

2 All your works praise you, O Lord,
and your faithful servants bless you.

3 They tell of the glory of your kingdom
and speak of your mighty power,

4 To make known to all peoples your mighty acts
and the glorious splendour of your kingdom.

5 Your kingdom is an everlasting kingdom;
your dominion endures throughout all ages.

6 The Lord is sure in all his words
and faithful in all his deeds.

**Glory to the Father, and to the Son,
and to the Holy Spirit;
as it was in the beginning, is now,
and shall be for ever. Amen.**

N. T. reading

Canticle

Venite – a Song of Triumph

Antiphon: **O come, let us sing**

1 O come, let us sing to the Lord;
   let us heartily rejoice in the rock of our salvation.

2 Let us come into his presence with thanksgiving
   and be glad in him with psalms.

3 For the Lord is a great God
   and a great king above all gods.

4 In his hand are the depths of the earth
   and the heights of the mountains are his also.

5 The sea is his, for he made it,
   and his hands have moulded the dry land.

6 Come, let us worship and bow down
   and kneel before the Lord our Maker.

7 For he is our God;
   we are the people of his pasture and the sheep of his hand.

**Glory to the Father, and to the Son,
and to the Holy Spirit;
as it was in the beginning, is now,
and shall be for ever. Amen.**

Antiphon: **O come, let us sing to the Lord**

The Prayers

The Kyries

Lord, have mercy.
Christ, have mercy.
Lord, have mercy.

The Lord's Prayer

Our Father in heaven,
hallowed be your name,
your kingdom come,
your will be done,
on earth as in heaven.
Give us today our daily bread.
Forgive us our sins
as we forgive those who sin against us.
Lead us not into temptation
but deliver us from evil.
[For the kingdom, the power,
and the glory are yours
now and for ever.] Amen.

Blessed are all those who fear the Lord,
and walk in his ways.

You shall eat the fruit of the toil of your hands;
it shall go well with you, and happy shall you be.

O Lord, hear our prayer
and let our cry come to you.

The Collect of the day, or the following:

O God, whose beauty is beyond our imagining
and whose power we cannot comprehend:
show us your glory as far as we can grasp it,
and shield us from knowing more than we can bear
until we may look upon you without fear;
through Jesus Christ our Saviour.
Amen.

Silent prayer

Conclusion

O Lord, hear our prayer
and let our cry come to you.

Let us bless the Lord.
Thanks be to God.

The grace of our Lord Jesus Christ,
and the love of God,
and the fellowship of the Holy Spirit,
be with us all evermore.
Amen.

MIDDAY PRAYER

Saturday

O God, make speed to save us.
O Lord, make haste to help us.

**Glory to the Father, and to the Son,
and to the Holy Spirit;
as it was in the beginning, is now,
and shall be for ever. Amen.**

Hymn

**Like a mighty river flowing,
like a flower in beauty growing,
far beyond all human knowing
is the perfect peace of God.**

**Like the hills serene and even,
like the coursing clouds of heaven,
like the heart that's been forgiven
is the perfect peace of God.**

**Like the summer breezes playing,
like the tall trees softly swaying,
like the lips of silent praying
is the perfect peace of God.**

**Like the morning sun ascended,
like the scents of evening blended,
like a friendship never ended
is the perfect peace of God.**

**Like the azure ocean swelling,
like the jewel all-excelling,
far beyond our human telling
is the perfect peace of God.**

Psalm 145.1–10

Antiphon: **Great is the Lord**

1 I will exalt you, O God my King,
   and bless your name for ever and ever.

2 Every day will I bless you
   and praise your name for ever and ever.

3 Great is the Lord and highly to be praised;
   his greatness is beyond all searching out.

4 One generation shall praise your works to another
   and declare your mighty acts.

5 They shall speak of the majesty of your glory,
   and I will tell of all your wonderful deeds.

6 They shall speak of the might of your marvellous acts,
   and I will also tell of your greatness.

7 They shall pour forth the story of your abundant
       kindness
   and joyfully sing of your righteousness.

8 The Lord is gracious and merciful,
   long-suffering and of great goodness.

9 The Lord is loving to everyone
   and his mercy is over all his creatures.

10 All your works praise you, O Lord,
   and your faithful servants bless you.

**Glory to the Father, and to the Son,
and to the Holy Spirit;
as it was in the beginning, is now,
and shall be for ever. Amen.**

Antiphon: **Great is the Lord and highly to be praised**

Chapter
Isaiah 40.27–31

Why do you say, O Jacob, and complain, O Israel, 'My way is hidden from the Lord; my cause is disregarded by my God'? Do you not know? Have you not heard? The Lord is the everlasting God, the Creator of the ends of the earth. He will not grow tired or weary, and his understanding no one can fathom. He gives strength to the weary and increases the power of the weak. Even youths grow tired and weary, and young men stumble and fall; but those who hope in the Lord will renew their strength. They will soar on wings like eagles; they will run and not grow weary, they will walk and not be faint.

Thanks be to God.

Canticle
Habakkuk 3.17–19

Antiphon: **He enables me**

1 Though the fig-tree does not bud
  and there are no grapes on the vines,

2 Though the olive crop fails
  and the fields produce no food,

3 Though there are no sheep in the pen
  and no cattle in the stalls

4 Yet I will rejoice in the Lord,
  I will be joyful in God my Saviour.

5 The Sovereign Lord is my strength;
   he makes my feet like the feet of a deer,
  he enables me to go on the heights.

Antiphon: **He enables me to go on the heights**

The Prayers

The Kyries

Lord, have mercy.
Christ, have mercy.
Lord, have mercy.

The Lord's Prayer

Our Father in heaven,
hallowed be your name,
your kingdom come,
your will be done,
on earth as in heaven.
Give us today our daily bread.
Forgive us our sins
as we forgive those who sin against us.
Lead us not into temptation
but deliver us from evil.
[For the kingdom, the power,
and the glory are yours
now and for ever.] Amen.

Hear my prayer, O God.
Give heed to the words of my mouth.

In the evening and morning and at noonday
I will pray and make my supplication.

I will call upon the Most High God,
the God who fulfils his purpose for me.

Be exalted, O God, above the heavens,
and your glory over all the earth.

The Collect of the day, or the following:

Almighty God,
you have taught us through your Son
that love is the fulfilling of the law:
grant that we may love you with our whole heart
and our neighbours as ourselves;
through Jesus Christ our Lord.
Amen.

Conclusion

O Lord, hear our prayer
and let our cry come to you.

Let us bless the Lord.
Thanks be to God.

May God bless our times of rest and recreation.
Amen.

EVENING PRAYER

Saturday

O Lord, open our lips
and our mouth shall proclaim your praise.

Answer me when I call,
O God of my righteousness.

Glory to the Father, and to the Son,
and to the Holy Spirit;
as it was in the beginning, is now,
and shall be for ever. Amen.

Evening hymn

At evening, when the sun had set,
the sick, O Lord, around you lay:
in what distress and pain they met,
but in what joy they went away!

Once more the evening comes, and we
oppressed with various ills draw near;
and though your form we cannot see,
we know and feel that you are here.

O Saviour Christ, our fears dispel –
for some are sick and some are sad,
and some have never loved you well,
and some have lost the love they had.

And none, O Lord, have perfect rest,
for none are wholly free from sin;
and those who long to serve you best
are conscious most of wrong within.

O Saviour Christ, the Son of Man,
you have been troubled, tested, tried;
your kind but searching glance can scar
the very wounds that shame would hide.

Your touch has still its ancient power;
no word from you can fruitless fall:
meet with us in this evening hour
and in your mercy heal us all!

Psalm 104.26–33

Antiphon: **May the glory of the Lord**

1 O Lord, how manifold are your works!
In wisdom you have made them all;
   the earth is full of your creatures.

2 There is the sea, spread far and wide,
and there move creatures beyond number, both small and
   great.

3 There go the ships, and there is that Leviathan
which you have made to play in the deep.

4 All of these look to you
to give them their food in due season.

5 When you give it them, they gather it;
you open your hand and they are filled with good.

6 When you hide your face they are troubled;
when you take away their breath,
   they die and return again to the dust.

7 When you send forth your spirit, they are created,
and you renew the face of the earth.

8 May the glory of the Lord endure for ever;
may the Lord rejoice in his works;

**Glory to the Father, and to the Son,
and to the Holy Spirit;
as it was in the beginning, is now,
and shall be for ever. Amen.**

Antiphon: **May the glory of the Lord endure for ever**

Chapter
1 Peter 3.8–9

Finally, all of you, live in harmony with one another; be sympathetic, love as brothers, be compassionate and humble. Do not repay evil with evil or insult with insult, but with blessing, because to this you were called so that you may inherit a blessing.

Thanks be to God.

Lectionary readings – *if you have time, one or both*

O. T. reading

Magnificat – The Song of Mary
Luke 1.46–55

Antiphon: **He has mercy**

1 My soul proclaims the greatness of the Lord;
  my spirit rejoices in God my Saviour.

2 For he has looked with favour on his lowly servant;
  from this day all generations will call me blessed.

3 The Almighty has done great things for me,
  and holy is his name.

4 He has mercy on those who fear him
  in every generation.

5 He has shown the strength of his arm;
  he has scattered the proud in their conceit.

6 He has cast down the mighty from their thrones
  and has lifted up the lowly.

7 He has filled the hungry with good things
  and the rich he has sent away empty.

8 He has come to the help of his servant, Israel,
  for he has remembered his promise of mercy.

9 The promise he made to our forebears,
  to Abraham and his children for ever.

Glory to the Father, and to the Son,
and to the Holy Spirit;
as it was in the beginning, is now,
and shall be for ever. Amen.

Antiphon: **He has mercy on those who fear him**

N. T. reading

The Prayers

I will sing to the Lord as long as I live.
I will make music to my God while I have my being.

The Kyries

Lord, have mercy.
Christ, have mercy.
Lord, have mercy.

The Lord's Prayer

Our Father in heaven,
hallowed be your name,
your kingdom come,
your will be done,
on earth as in heaven.
Give us today our daily bread.
Forgive us our sins
as we forgive those who sin against us.
Lead us not into temptation
but deliver us from evil.
[For the kingdom, the power,
and the glory are yours
now and for ever.] Amen.

I will exalt you, O God my king,
and bless your name for ever and ever.

Every day will I bless you
and praise your name for ever and ever.

Great is the Lord
and highly to be praised.

The Collect of the day, or the following:

Teach us, good Lord, to serve you as you deserve;
to give and not to count the cost;
to fight and not to heed the wounds;
to toil and not to seek for rest;
to labour and not to seek for any reward,
save that of knowing that we do your will;
through Jesus Christ our Lord.
Amen.

Silent prayer

Conclusion

The grace of our Lord Jesus Christ,
and the love of God,
and the fellowship of the Holy Spirit,
be with us all evermore.
Amen.

Let us bless the Lord.
Thanks be to God.

AN ORDER FOR COMPLINE
(A Late Evening Service)

Saturday

The Lord Almighty grant us a quiet night and a perfect end.
Amen.

Be self-controlled and alert. Your enemy the devil prowls
around like a roaring lion looking for someone to devour.
Resist him, standing firm in the faith.

(1 Peter 5.8–9)

But you, O Lord, have mercy upon us.
Thanks be to God.

O God, make speed to save us.
O Lord, make haste to help us.

Glory to the Father, and to the Son,
and to the Holy Spirit;
as it was in the beginning, is now,
and shall be for ever. Amen.

Praise to the Lord.
The Lord's name be praised.

Psalm 116.6–12

1 Turn again to your rest, O my soul,
  for the Lord has been gracious to you.

2 For you have delivered my soul from death,
  my eyes from tears and my feet from falling.

3 I will walk before the Lord
  in the land of the living.

4 I believed that I should perish
    for I was sorely troubled;
  and I said in my alarm,
    'Everyone is a liar.'

5 How shall I repay the Lord
  for all the benefits he has given to me?

6 I will lift up the cup of salvation
  and call upon the name of the Lord.

7 I will fulfil my vows to the Lord
  in the presence of all his people.

Short lesson

No good tree bears bad fruit, nor does a bad tree bear good
fruit. Each tree is recognized by its own fruit. People do not
pick figs from thorn-bushes, or grapes from briers. The good
man brings good things out of the good stored up in his
heart, and the evil man brings evil things out of the evil
stored up in his heart. For out of the overflow of his heart
his mouth speaks.

(Luke 6.43–45)

Hymn

Sun of my soul, thou Saviour dear,
it is not night if thou be near:
O may no earth-born cloud arise
to hide thee from thy servant's eyes.

When the soft dews of kindly sleep
my wearied eyelids gently steep,
be my last thought, how sweet to rest
for ever on my Saviour's breast.

Abide with me from morn till eve,
for without thee I cannot live;
abide with me when night is nigh,
for without thee I dare not die.

Watch by the sick; enrich the poor
with blessings from thy boundless store;
be ev'ry mourner's sleep tonight
like infants slumbers, pure and light.

Antiphon: **Preserve us, O Lord, while waking, and guard us while sleeping, that awake we may watch with Christ, and asleep we may rest in peace.**

The Prayers

The Kyries

Lord, have mercy.
Christ, have mercy.
Lord, have mercy.

The Lord's Prayer

**Our Father in heaven,
hallowed be your name,
your kingdom come,
your will be done,
on earth as in heaven.
Give us today our daily bread.
Forgive us our sins
as we forgive those who sin against us.
Lead us not into temptation
but deliver us from evil.
[For the kingdom, the power,
and the glory are yours
now and for ever.] Amen.**

I will bless the Lord who has given me counsel,
and in the night watches he instructs my heart.

I have set the Lord always before me.
He is at my right hand; I shall not fall.

Weigh my heart, examine me by night.
Refine me, and you will find no impurity in me.

We confess to God Almighty,
the Father, the Son, and the Holy Spirit,
that we have sinned in thought, word, and deed,
through our own grievous fault.
Therefore we pray God to have mercy upon us.

Almighty God, have mercy upon us,
forgive us all our sins and deliver us from all evil,
confirm and strengthen us in all goodness,
and bring us to life everlasting;
through Jesus Christ our Lord.
Amen.

Will you not give us life again, O Lord:
that your people may rejoice in you?

Show us your mercy, O Lord,
and grant us your salvation.

Keep us tonight, Lord, from all sin.
Have mercy on us, Lord, have mercy.

Lord, hear our prayer
and let our cry come to you.

Collect

Almighty God, give us wisdom to perceive you,
intellect to understand you,
diligence to seek you,
patience to wait for you,
vision to behold you,
a heart to meditate upon you,
and life to proclaim you.
Amen.

(St Benedict)

Nunc Dimittis

1 Now, Lord, you let your servant go in peace:
  your word has been fulfilled.

2 My own eyes have seen the salvation
  which you have prepared in the sight of every people:

3 A light to reveal you to the nations
  and the glory of your people Israel.

Glory to the Father, and to the Son,
and to the Holy Spirit;
as it was in the beginning, is now,
and shall be for ever. Amen.

We will lay us down in peace and take our rest,
for it is you, Lord, only who make us dwell in safety.

The Lord be with you
and with your spirit.

Let us bless the Lord.
Thanks be to God.

The Almighty and merciful Lord,
the Father, the Son, and the Holy Spirit,
bless and preserve us. Amen.

The Lectionary

Readings for daily morning prayer

	JANUARY	First Lesson	Second Lesson
1	*Circumcision*	Gen. 17.9–end	Rom. 2.17–end
2		Gen.1.1–19	Matt. 1.18–end
3		Gen. 2.4–end	Matt. 2
4		Gen. 3.20–4.15	Matt. 3
5		Gen. 5.1–27	Matt. 4.1–22
6	*Epiphany*	Isa. 60	Luke 3.15–23
7		Gen. 6.9–end	Matt. 4.23–5.12
8		Gen. 8	Matt. 5.13–32
9		Gen. 11.1–9	Matt. 5.33–end
10		Gen. 13	Matt. 6.1–18
11		Gen. 15	Matt. 6.19–7.6
12		Gen. 17.1–23	Matt. 7.7–end
13		Gen. 18.17–end	Matt. 8.1–17
14		Gen. 20	Matt. 8.18–end
15		Gen. 21.33–22.19	Matt. 9.1–17
16		Gen. 24.1–28	Matt. 9.18–end
17		Gen. 24.52–end	Matt. 10.1–23
18		Gen. 25.19–end	Matt. 10.24–end
19		Gen. 26.18–end	Matt. 11
20		Gen. 27.30–end	Matt. 12.1–21
21		Gen. 29.1–21	Matt. 12.22–end
22		Gen. 31.36–end	Matt. 13.1–23
23		Gen. 32.22–end	Matt. 13.24–52
24		Gen. 35.1–21	Matt. 13.53–14.12
25	*Conv. of St Paul*	Isa. 49.1–13	Gal. 1.11–end
26		Gen. 37.12–end	Matt. 14.13–end
27		Gen. 40	Matt. 15.1–20
28		Gen. 41.17–52	Matt. 15.21–end
29		Gen. 42.25–end	Matt. 16.1–23
30		Gen. 43.25–44.13	Matt. 16.24–17.13
31		Gen. 45.1–24	Matt. 17.14–end

Readings for daily evening prayer

JANUARY	First Lesson	Second Lesson
1 *Circumcision*	Deut. 10.12–end	Col 2.8–17
2	Gen. 1.20–2.3	Acts 1
3	Gen. 3.1–19	Acts 2.1–21
4	Gen. 4.16–end	Acts 2.22–end
5	Gen. 5.28–6.8	Acts 3
6 *Epiphany*	Isa. 49.13–24	John 2.1–11
7	Gen. 7	Acts 4.1–31
8	Gen. 9.1–19	Acts 4.32–5.16
9	Gen. 12	Acts 5.17–end
10	Gen. 14	Acts 6
11	Gen. 16	Acts 7.1–34
12	Gen. 18.1–16	Acts 7.35–8.4
13	Gen. 19.12–29	Acts 8.5–25
14	Gen. 21.1–21	Acts 8.26–end
15	Gen. 23	Acts 9.1–22
16	Gen. 24.29–51	Acts 9.23–end
17	Gen. 25.5–18	Acts 10.1–23
18	Gen. 26.1–17	Acts 10.24–end
19	Gen. 27.1–29	Acts 11
20	Gen. 28	Acts 12
21	Gen. 31.1–24	Acts 13.1–25
22	Gen. 32.1–21	Acts 13.26–end
23	Gen. 33	Acts 14
24	Gen. 37.1–11	Acts 15.1–29
25 *Conv. of St Paul*	Jer. 1.1–10	Acts 26.1–20
26	Gen. 39	Acts 15.30–16.15
27	Gen. 41.1–16	Acts 16.16–end
28	Gen. 41.53–42.24	Acts 17.1–15
29	Gen. 43.1–24	Acts 17.16–end
30	Gen. 44.14–end	Acts 13.1–23
31	Gen. 45.25–46.7	Acts 18.24–19.20

Readings for daily morning prayer

FEBRUARY	First Lesson	Second Lesson
1	Gen. 46.26–47.12	Matt. 18.1–20
2 *Purif. of V. Mary*	Exod. 13.1–16	Matt. 18.21–19.2
3	Gen. 48	Matt. 19.3–26
4	Gen. 50	Matt. 19.27–20.16
5	Exod. 2	Matt. 20.17–end
6	Exod. 4.1–23	Matt. 21.1–22
7	Exod. 5.15–6.13	Matt. 21.23–end
8	Exod. 7.14–end	Matt. 22.1–14
9	Exod. 8.20–9.12	Matt. 22.15–40
10	Exod. 10.1–20	Matt. 22.41–23.12
11	Exod. 12.1–20	Matt. 23.13–end
12	Exod. 12.43–13.16	Matt. 24.1–28
13	Exod. 14.10–end	Matt. 24.29–end
14	Exod. 15.22–16.10	Matt. 25.1–30
15	Exod. 17	Matt. 25.31–end
16	Exod. 19	Matt. 26.1–30
17	Exod. 21.1–17	Matt. 26.31–56
18	Exod. 23.14–end	Matt. 26.57–end
19	Exod. 25.1–22	Matt. 27.1–26
20	Exod. 28.29–41	Matt. 27.27–56
21	Exod. 31	Matt. 27.57–end
22	Exod. 32.15–end	Matt. 28
23	Exod. 33.12–34.9	Mark 1.1–20
24 *St Matthias, Ap*	1 Sam. 2.27–35	Mark 1.21–end
25	Exod. 34.27–end	Mark 2.1–22
26	Exod. 39.30–end	Mark 2.23–3.12
27	Exod. 40.17–end	Mark 3.13–end
28	Lev. 14.1–22	Mark 4.1–34
29	Lev. 19.1–18	Matt. 7

FEBRUARY	First Lesson	Second Lesson
1	Gen. 47.13–end	Acts 19.21–end
2 *Purif. of V. Mary*	Haggai 2.1–9	Acts 20.1–16
3	Gen. 49	Acts 20.17–end
4	Exod. 1	Acts 21.1–16
5	Exod. 3	Acts 21.17–36
6	Exod. 4.27–5.14	Acts 21.37–22.21
7	Exod. 6.28–7.13	Acts 22.22–23.11
8	Exod. 8.1–19	Acts 23.12–end
9	Exod. 9.13–end	Acts 24
10	Exod. 10.21–11.10	Acts 25
11	Exod. 12.21–42	Acts 26
12	Exod. 13.17–14.9	Acts 27.1–17
13	Exod. 15.1–21	Acts 27.18–end
14	Exod. 16.11–end	Acts 28.1–16
15	Exod. 18	Acts 28.17–end
16	Exod. 20.1–21	Rom. 1
17	Exod. 22.21–23.9	Rom. 2.1–16
18	Exod. 24	Rom. 2.17–end
19	Exod. 28.1–12	Rom. 3
20	Exod. 29.35–30.10	Rom. 4
21	Exod. 32.1–14	Rom. 5
22	Exod. 33.1–11	Rom. 6
23	Exod. 34.10–26	Rom. 7
24 *St Matthias, Ap*	Isa. 22.15–end	Rom. 8.1–17
25	Exod. 35.29–36.7	Rom. 8.18–end
26	Exod. 40.1–16	Rom. 9.1–18
27	Lev. 9.22–10.11	Rom. 9.19–end
28	Lev. 16.1–22	Rom. 10
29	Lev. 19.30–20.8	Rom. 12

Readings for daily morning prayer

MARCH	First Lesson	Second Lesson
1	Lev. 25.1–17	Mark 4.35–5.20
2	Lev. 26.1–20	Mark 5.21–end
3	Num. 6	Mark 6.1–13
4	Num. 10.11–end	Mark 6.14–29
5	Num. 11.24–end	Mark 6.30–end
6	Num. 13.17–end	Mark 7.1–23
7	Num. 14.26–end	Mark 7.24–8.9
8	Num. 16.23–end	Mark 8.10–9.1
9	Num. 20.1–13	Mark 9.2–29
10	Num. 21.1–9	Mark 9.30–end
11	Num. 22.1–21	Mark 10.1–31
12	Num. 23	Mark 10.32–end
13	Num. 25	Mark 11.1–26
14	Deut. 1.1–18	Mark 11.27–12.12
15	Deut. 2.1–25	Mark 12.13–34
16	Deut. 3.18–end	Mark 12.35–13.13
17	Deut. 4.25–40	Mark 13.14–end
18	Deut. 5.22–end	Mark 14.1–26
19	Deut. 7.1–11	Mark 14.27–52
20	Deut. 8	Mark 14.53–end
21	Deut. 11.1–17	Mark 15.1–41
22	Deut. 15.1–15	Mark 15.42–16.20
23	Deut. 18.9–end	Luke 1.1–25
24	Deut. 26	Luke 1.26–45
25 *Annune, of V. Mary*	Gen. 3.1–15	Luke 1.46–end
26	Deut. 28.1–14	Luke 2.1–20
27	Deut. 28.47–end	Luke 2.21–end
28	Deut. 30	Luke 3.1–22
29	Deut. 31.14–29	Luke 4.1–15
30	Deut. 32.44–end	Luke 4.16–end
31	Deut. 34	Luke 5.1–16

Readings for daily evening prayer

MARCH		First Lesson	Second Lesson
1		Lev. 25.18–43	Rom. 11.1–24
2		Lev. 26.21–end	Rom. 11.25–end
3		Num. 9.15–10.10	Rom. 12
4		Num. 11.1–23	Rom. 13
5		Num. 12	Rom. 14–15.7
6		Num. 14.1–25	Rom. 15.8–end
7		Num. 16.1–22	Rom. 16
8		Num. 17	1 Cor. 1.1–25
9		Num. 20.14–end	1 Cor. 1.26–2.16
10		Num. 21.10–31	1 Cor. 3
11		Num. 22.22–end	1 Cor. 4.1–17
12		Num. 24	1 Cor. 4.18–5.13
13		Num. 27.12–end	1 Cor. 6
14		Deut. 1.19–end	1 Cor. 7.1–24
15		Deut. 2.26–3.17	1 Cor. 7.25–end
16		Deut. 4.1–24	1 Cor. 8
17		Deut. 5.1–21	1 Cor. 9
18		Deut. 6	1 Cor. 10–11.1
19		Deut. 7.12–end	1 Cor. 11.2–16
20		Deut. 10.8–end	1 Cor. 11.17–end
21		Deut. 11.18–end	1 Cor. 12.1–27
22		Deut. 17.8–end	1 Cor. 12.28–13.13
23		Deut. 24.5–end	1 Cor. 14.1–19
24		Deut. 27	1 Cor. 14.20–end
25	*Annune, of V. Mary*	Isa. 52.7–12	1 Cor. 15.1–34
26		Deut. 28.15–46	1 Cor. 15.35–end
27		Deut. 29.9–end	1 Cor. 16
28		Deut. 31.1–13	2 Cor. 1.1–22
29		Deut. 31.30–32.43	2 Cor. 1.23–2.13
30		Deut. 33	2 Cor. 2.14–3.18
31		Josh. 1	2 Cor. 4

Readings for daily morning prayer

APRIL	First Lesson	Second Lesson
1	Josh. 2	Luke 5.17–end
2	Josh. 4	Luke 6.1–19
3	Josh. 6	Luke 6.20–end
4	Josh. 9.3–end	Luke 7.1–23
5	Josh. 21.43–22.9	Luke 7.24–end
6	Josh. 23	Luke 8.1–25
7	Judges 2	Luke 8.26–end
8	Judges 5	Luke 9.1–27
9	Judges 6.25–end	Luke 9.28–50
10	Judges 8.32–9.24	Luke 9.51–10.16
11	Judges 11.1–28	Luke 10.17–end
12	Judges 13	Luke 11.1–28
13	Judges 15	Luke 11.29–end
14	Ruth 1	Luke 12.1–34
15	Ruth 3	Luke 12.35–end
16	1 Sam. 1	Luke 13.1–17
17	1 Sam. 2.21–end	Luke 13.18–end
18	1 Sam. 4	Luke 14.1–24
19	1 Sam. 6	Luke 14.25–15.10
20	1 Sam. 8	Luke 15.11–end
21	1 Sam. 10	Luke 16
22	1 Sam. 12	Luke 17.1–19
23	1 Sam. 14.1–23	Luke 17.20–end
24	1 Sam. 15	Luke 18.1–30
25 *St Mark, Evang*	Isa. 62.6–end	Luke 18.31–19.10
26	1 Sam. 17.1–30	Luke 19.11–27
27	1 Sam. 17.55–18.16	Luke 19.28–end
28	1 Sam. 20.1–17	Luke 20.1–26
29	1 Sam. 21	Luke 20.27–21.4
30	1 Sam. 23	Luke 21.5–end

Readings for daily evening prayer

APRIL	First Lesson	Second Lesson
1	Josh. 3	2 Cor. 5
2	Josh. 5	2 Cor. 6–7.1
3	Josh. 7	2 Cor. 7.2–end
4	Josh. 10.1–15	2 Cor. 8
5	Josh. 22.10–end	2 Cor. 9
6	Josh. 24	2 Cor. 10
7	Judges 4	2 Cor. 11.1–29
8	Judges 6.1–24	2 Cor. 11.30–12.13
9	Judges 7	2 Cor. 12.14–13.14
10	Judges 10	Gal. 1
11	Judges 11.29–end	Gal. 2
12	Judges 14	Gal. 3
13	Judges 16	Gal. 4.1–20
14	Ruth 2	Gal. 4.21–5.12
15	Ruth 4	Gal. 5.13–end
16	1 Sam. 2.1–20	Gal. 6
17	1 Sam. 3	Eph. 1
18	1 Sam. 5	Eph. 2
19	1 Sam. 7	Eph. 3
20	1 Sam. 9	Eph. 4.1–24
21	1 Sam. 11	Eph. 4.25–5.21
22	1 Sam. 13	Eph. 5.22–6.9
23	1 Sam. 14.24–46	Eph. 6.10–end
24	1 Sam. 16	Phil. 1
25 *St Mark, Evang*	Ezek. 1.1–14	Phil. 2
26	1 Sam. 17.31–54	Phil. 3
27	1 Sam. 19	Phil. 4
28	1 Sam. 20.18–end	Col. 1.1–20
29	1 Sam. 22	Col. 1.21–2.7
30	1 Sam. 24–25.1	Col. 2.8–end

Readings for daily morning prayer

MAY		First Lesson	Second Lesson
1	*St Philip & St James*	Isa. 61	John 1.1–42
2		1 Sam. 26	Luke 22.1–30
3		1 Sam. 31	Luke 22.31–53
4		2 Sam. 3.17–end	Luke 22.54–end
5		2 Sam. 6	Luke 23.1–25
6		2 Sam. 7.18–end	Luke 23.26–49
7		2 Sam. 11	Luke 23.50–24.12
8		2 Sam. 13.38–14.25	Luke 24.13–end
9		2 Sam. 15.16–end	John 1.1–28
10		2 Sam. 16.15–17.23	John 1.29–end
11		2 Sam. 18.18–end	John 2
12		2 Sam. 19.24–end	John 3.1–21
13		2 Sam. 23.1–23	John 3.22–end
14		1 Kings 1.1–27	John 4.1–30
15		1 Chron. 29.10–end	John 4.31–end
16		1 Kings 4.20–end	John 5.1–23
17		1 Kings 6.1–14	John 5.24–end
18		1 Kings 8.22–53	John 6.1–21
19		1 Kings 10	John 6.22–40
20		1 Kings 11.26–end	John 6.41–end
21		1 Kings 12.25–13.10	John 7.1–24
22		1 Kings 14.1–20	John 7.25–end
23		1 Kings 16.8–end	John 8.1–30
24		1 Kings 18.1–16	John 8.31–end
25		1 Kings 19	John 9.1–38
26		1 Kings 22.1–40	John 9.39–10.21
27		2 Kings 2	John 10.22–end
28		2 Kings 5	John 11.1–16
29		2 Kings 6.24–end	John 11.17–46
30		2 Kings 8.1–15	John 11.47–12.19
31		2 Kings 10.1–17	John 12.20–end

Readings for daily evening prayer

MAY		First Lesson	Second Lesson
1	*St Philip & St James*	Zech. 4	Col. 3.1–17
2		1 Sam. 28.3–end	Col. 3.18–4.6
3		2 Sam. 1	Col. 4.7–end
4		2 Sam. 4	1 Thess. 1
5		2 Sam. 7.1–17	1 Thess. 2
6		2 Sam. 9	1 Thess. 3
7		2 Sam. 12.1–23	1 Thess. 4
8		2 Sam. 15.1–15	1 Thess. 5
9		2 Sam. 16.1–14	2 Thess. 1
10		2 Sam. 17.24–18.17	2 Thess. 2
11		2 Sam. 19.1–23	2 Thess. 3
12		2 Sam. 21.1–14	1 Tim. 1.1–17
13		2 Sam. 24	1 Tim. 1.18–2.15
14		1 Kings 1.28–48	1 Tim. 3
15		1 Kings 3	1 Tim. 4
16		1 Kings 5	1 Tim. 5
17		1 Kings 8.1–21	1 Tim. 6
18		1 Kings 8.54–9.9	2 Tim. 1
19		1 Kings 11.1–25	2 Tim. 2
20		1 Kings 12.1–24	2 Tim. 3
21		1 Kings 13.11–end	2 Tim. 4
22		1 Kings 15.25–16.7	Titus 1
23		1 Kings 17	Titus 2
24		1 Kings 18.17–end	Titus 3
25		1 Kings 21	Philemon
26		2 Kings 1	Heb. 1
27		2 Kings 4.8–end	Heb. 2–3.6
28		2 Kings 6.1–23	Heb. 3.7–4.13
29		2 Kings 7	Heb. 4.14–5.14
30		2 Kings 9	Heb. 6
31		2 Kings 10.18–end	Heb. 7

Readings for daily morning prayer

JUNE		First Lesson	Second Lesson
1		2 Kings 13	John 13.1–20
2		2 Kings 17.24–end	John 13.21–end
3		2 Chron. 13	John 14
4		2 Chron. 15	John 15
5		2 Chron. 19	John 16.1–15
6		2 Chron. 20.31–21.20	John 16.16–end
7		2 Chron. 23	John 17
8		2 Chron. 25	John 18.1–27
9		2 Chron. 28	John 18.28–end
10		2 Chron. 29.3–20	John 19.1–24
11	*St Barnabas, Ap*	Deut. 33.1–11	Acts 4.31–end
12		2 Kings 18.13–end	John 19.25–end
13		2 Kings 19.20–end	John 20.1–18
14		Isa. 38.9–20	John 20.19–end
15		2 Kings 22	John 21
16		2 Kings 23.21–24.7	Acts 1
17		2 Kings 25.8–end	Acts 2.1–21
18		Ezra 4	Acts 2.22–end
19		Ezra 7	Acts 3
20		Ezra 9	Acts 4.1–31
21		Neh. 1	Acts 4.32–5.16
22		Neh. 4	Acts 5.17–end
23		Neh. 6–7.4	Acts 6
24	*St John Baptist*	Mal. 3.1–6	Matt. 3
25		Neh.13.1–14	Acts 7.1–34
26		Esther 1	Acts 7.35–8.4
27		Esther 4	Acts 8.5–25
28		Esther 6	Acts 8.26–end
29	*St Peter, Ap*	Ezek. 3.4–14	John 21.15–22
30		Job 1	Acts 9.1–22

Readings for daily evening prayer

JUNE		First Lesson	Second Lesson
1		2 Kings 17.1–23	Heb. 8
2		2 Chron. 12	Heb. 9
3		2 Chron. 14	Heb. 10.1–18
4		2 Chron. 16–17.13	Heb. 10.19–end
5		2 Chron. 20.1–30	Heb. 11.1–16
6		2 Chron. 22	Heb. 11.17–end
7		2 Chron. 24	Heb. 12
8		2 Chron. 26–27.9	Heb. 13
9		2 Kings 18.1–8	James 1
10		2 Chron.30–31.1	James 2
11	*St Barnabas, Ap*	Nahum 1	Acts 14.8–end
12		2 Kings 19.1–19	James 3
13		2 Kings 20	James 4
14		2 Chron. 33	James 5
15		2 Kings 23.1–20	1 Peter 1.1–21
16		2 Kings 24.8–25.7	1 Peter 1.22–2.10
17		Ezra 1–3.13	1 Peter 2.11–3.7
18		Ezra 5	1 Peter 3.8–4.6
19		Ezra 8.15–end	1 Peter 4.7–end
20		Ezra 10.1–19	1 Peter 5
21		Neh. 2	2 Peter 1
22		Neh. 5	2 Peter 2
23		Neh. 7.73–8.18	2 Peter 3
24	*St John Baptist*	Mal. 4	Matt. 14.1–12
25		Neh.13.15–end	1 John 1
26		Esther 2.15–3.15	1 John 2.1–14
27		Esther 5	1 John 2.15–end
28		Esther 7	1 John 3.1–15
29	*St Peter, Ap*	Zech. 3	Acts 4.8–22
30		Job 2	1 John 3.16–4.6

Readings for Daily Morning Prayer

JULY	First Lesson	Second Lesson
1	Job 3	Acts 9.23–end
2	Job 5	Acts 10.1–23
3	Job 7	Acts 10.24–end
4	Job 10	Acts 11
5	Job 12	Acts 12
6	Job 14	Acts 13.1–25
7	Job 17	Acts 13.26–end
8	Job 21	Acts 14
9	Job 23	Acts 15.1–29
10	Job 25–26.14	Acts 15.30–16.15
11	Job 28	Acts 16.16–end
12	Job 30.12–26	Acts 17.1–15
13	Job 32	Acts 17.16–end
14	Job 38.39–39.30	Acts 18.1–23
15	Job 41	Acts 18.24–19.20
16	Prov. 1.1–19	Acts 19.21–end
17	Prov. 2	Acts 20.1–16
18	Prov. 3.27–4.19	Acts 20.17–end
19	Prov. 5.15–end	Acts 21.1–16
20	Prov. 7	Acts 21.17–36
21	Prov. 9	Acts 21.37–22.22
22	Prov. 11.1–14	Acts 22.23–23.11
23	Prov. 12.10–end	Acts 23.12–end
24	Prov. 14.9–27	Acts 24
25 *St James, Ap*	2 Kings 1.1–15	Luke 9.51–56
26	Prov. 15.18–end	Acts 25
27	Prov. 16.31–17.17	Acts 26
28	Prov. 19.13–end	Acts 27
29	Prov. 21.1–16	Acts 28.1–16
30	Prov. 23.10–end	Acts 28.17–end
31	Prov. 25	Rom. 1

Readings for Daily Evening Prayer

JULY	First Lesson	Second Lesson
1	Job 4	1 John 4.7–end
2	Job 6	1 John 5
3	Job 9	2 John
4	Job 11	3 John
5	Job 13	Jude
6	Job 16	Matt. 1.18–end
7	Job 19	Matt. 2
8	Job 22.12–28	Matt. 3
9	Job 24	Matt. 4.1–22
10	Job 27	Matt. 4.23–5.12
11	Job 29–30.1	Matt. 5.13–32
12	Job 31.13–end	Matt. 5.33–end
13	Job 38.1–38	Matt. 6.1–18
14	Job 40	Matt. 6.19–7.6
15	Job 42	Matt. 7.7–end
16	Prov. 1.20–end	Matt. 8.1–17
17	Prov. 3.1–26	Matt. 8.18–end
18	Prov. 4.20–5.14	Matt. 9.1–17
19	Prov. 6.1–19	Matt. 9.18–end
20	Prov. 8	Matt. 10.1–23
21	Prov. 10.16–end	Matt. 10.24–end
22	Prov. 11.15–end	Matt. 11
23	Prov. 13	Matt. 12.1–21
24	Prov. 14.28–15.17	Matt. 12.22–end
25 *St James, Ap*	Jer. 26.8–15	Matt. 13.1–23
26	Prov. 16.1–19	Matt. 13.24–52
27	Prov. 18.10–end	Matt. 13.53–14.12
28	Prov. 20.1–22	Matt. 14.13–end
29	Prov. 22.1–16	Matt. 15.1–20
30	Prov. 24.21–end	Matt. 15.21–end
31	Prov. 26.1–20	Matt. 16.1–23

Readings for Daily Morning Prayer

AUGUST	First Lesson	Second Lesson
1	Prov. 27.1–22	Rom. 2.1–16
2	Prov. 30.1–17	Rom. 2.17–end
3	Eccles. 1	Rom. 3
4	Eccles. 3	Rom. 4
5	Eccles. 5	Rom. 5
6 *Transfiguration*	Eccles. 7	Rom. 6
7	Eccles. 9	Rom. 7
8	Eccles. 12	Rom. 8.1–17
9	Jer. 2.1–13	Rom. 8.18–end
10	Jer. 5.19–end	Rom. 9.1–18
11	Jer. 7.1–16	Rom. 9.19–end
12	Jer. 9.1–16	Rom. 10
13	Jer. 15	Rom. 11.1–24
14	Jer. 18.1–17	Rom. 11.25–end
15	Jer. 21	Rom. 12
16	Jer. 22.13–end	Rom. 13
17	Jer. 24	Rom. 14–15.7
18	Jer. 26	Rom. 15.8–end
19	Jer. 29.4–19	Rom. 16
20	Jer. 31.1–14	1 Cor. 1.1–25
21	Jer. 33.1–13	1 Cor. 1.26–2.16
22	Jer. 35	1 Cor. 3
23	Jer. 36.14–end	1 Cor. 4.1–17
24 *St Bartholomew, Ap*	Gen. 28.10–17	1 Cor. 4.18–5.13
25	Jer. 38.14–end	1 Cor. 6
26	Jer. 50.1–20	1 Cor. 7.1–24
27	Ezek. 1.1–14	1 Cor. 7.25–end
28	Ezek. 2	1 Cor. 8
29	Ezek. 3.15–end	1 Cor. 9
30	Ezek. 9	1 Cor. 10–11.1
31	Ezek. 12.17–end	1 Cor. 11.2–16

Readings for Daily Evening Prayer

AUGUST		First Lesson	Second Lesson
1		Prov. 28.1–14	Matt. 16.24–17.13
2		Prov. 31.10–end	Matt. 17.14–end
3		Eccles. 2.1–11	Matt. 18.1–20
4		Eccles. 4	Matt. 18.21–19.2
5		Eccles. 6	Matt. 19.3–26
6	*Transfiguration*	Eccles. 8	Matt. 19.27–20.16
7		Eccles. 11	Matt. 20.17–end
8		Jer. 1	Matt. 21.1–22
9		Jer. 5.1–18	Matt. 21.23–end
10		Jer. 6.1–21	Matt. 22.1–14
11		Jer. 8.4–end	Matt. 22.15–40
12		Jer. 13.8–23	Matt. 22.41–23.12
13		Jer. 17.1–18	Matt. 23.13–end
14		Jer. 19	Matt. 24.1–28
15		Jer. 22.1–12	Matt. 24.29–end
16		Jer. 23.1–15	Matt. 25.1–30
17		Jer. 25.1–14	Matt. 25.31–end
18		Jer. 28	Matt. 26.1–30
19		Jer. 30	Matt. 26.31–56
20		Jer. 31.15–37	Matt. 26.57–end
21		Jer. 33.14–end	Matt. 27.1–26
22		Jer. 36.1–13	Matt. 27.27–56
23		Jer. 38.1–13	Matt. 27.57–end
24	*St Bartholomew, Ap*	Deut. 18.15–end	Matt. 28
25		Jer. 39	Mark 1.1–20
26		Jer. 51.54–end	Mark 1.21–end
27		Ezek. 1.15–end	Mark 2.1–22
28		Ezek. 3.1–14	Mark 2.23–3.12
29		Ezek. 8	Mark 3.13–end
30		Ezek. 11.14–end	Mark 4.1–34
31		Ezek. 13.1–16	Mark 4.35–5.20

Readings for Daily Morning Prayer

SEPTEMBER		First Lesson	Second Lesson
1		Ezek. 13.17–end	1 Cor. 11.17–end
2		Ezek. 14.12–end	1 Cor. 12.1–27
3		Ezek. 18.1–18	1 Cor. 12.28–13.13
4		Ezek. 20.1–17	1 Cor. 14.1–19
5		Ezek. 20.33–44	1 Cor. 14.20–end
6		Ezek. 24.15–end	1 Cor. 15.1–34
7		Ezek. 27.1–25	1 Cor. 15.35–end
8		Ezek. 28.1–19	1 Cor. 16
9		Ezek. 32.1–16	2 Cor. 1.1–22
10		Ezek. 33.21–end	2 Cor. 1.23–2.13
11		Ezek. 34.17–end	2 Cor. 2.14–3.18
12		Ezek. 37.1–14	2 Cor. 4
13		Ezek. 47.1–12	2 Cor. 5
14		Dan. 2.1–23	2 Cor. 6–7.1
15		Dan. 3	2 Cor. 7.2–end
16		Dan. 4.19–end	2 Cor. 8
17		Dan. 5.17–end	2 Cor. 9
18		Dan. 7.1–14	2 Cor. 10
19		Dan. 9.1–19	2 Cor. 11.1–29
20		Dan. 10.1–19	2 Cor. 11.30–12.13
21	*St Matthew, Ap*	1 Kings 19.15–end	2 Cor. 12.14–13.14
22		Hosea 2.14–end	Gal. 1
23		Hosea 5.8–6.6	Gal. 2
24		Hosea 8	Gal. 3
25		Hosea 10	Gal. 4.1–20
26		Hosea 13.1–14	Gal. 4.21–5.12
27		Joel 1	Gal. 5.13–end
28		Joel 2.15–27	Gal. 6
29	*St Michael & All Angels*	Gen. 32	Acts 12.5–17
30		Joel 3.1–8	Eph. 1

Readings for Daily Evening Prayer

SEPTEMBER		First Lesson	Second Lesson
1		Ezek. 14.1–11	Mark 5.21–end
2		Ezek. 16.44–end	Mark 6.1–13
3		Ezek. 18.19–end	Mark 6.14–29
4		Ezek. 20.18–32	Mark 6.30–end
5		Ezek. 22.23–end	Mark 7.1–23
6		Ezek. 26	Mark 7.24–8.9
7		Ezek. 27.26–end	Mark 8.10–9.1
8		Ezek. 31	Mark 9.2–29
9		Ezek. 33.1–20	Mark 9.30–end
10		Ezek. 34.1–16	Mark 10.1–31
11		Ezek. 36.16–32	Mark 10.32–end
12		Ezek. 37.15–end	Mark 11.1–26
13		Dan. 1	Mark 11.27–12.12
14		Dan. 2.24–end	Mark 12.13–34
15		Dan. 4.1–18	Mark 12.35–13.13
16		Dan. 5.1–16	Mark 13.14–end
17		Dan. 6	Mark 14.1–26
18		Dan. 7.15–end	Mark 14.27–52
19		Dan. 9.20–end	Mark 14.53–end
20		Dan. 12	Mark 15.1–41
21	*St Matthew, Ap*	1 Chron. 29.1–19	Mark 15.42–16.20
22		Hosea 4.1–12	Luke 1.1–25
23		Hosea 7.8–end	Luke 1.26–56
24		Hosea 9	Luke 1.57–end
25		Hosea 11–12.6	Luke 2.1–20
26		Hosea 14	Luke 2.21–end
27		Joel 2.1–14	Luke 3.1–22
28		Joel 2.28–3.8	Luke 4.1–15
29	*St Michael & All Angels*	Dan. 10.4–end	Rev. 14.14–end
30		Amos 1–2.3	Luke 4.16–end

OCTOBER	First Lesson	Second Lesson
1	Amos 2.4–3.8	Eph. 2
2	Amos 5.1–17	Eph. 3
3	Amos 7	Eph. 4.1–24
4	Amos 9	Eph. 4.25–5.21
5	Jonah 1	Eph. 5.22–6.9
6	Jonah 3	Eph. 6.10–end
7	Micah 1.1–9	Phil. 1
8	Micah 3	Phil. 2
9	Micah 5	Phil. 3
10	Micah 7	Phil. 4
11	Nahum 2	Col. 1.1–20
12	Hab. 1	Col. 1.21–2.7
13	Hab. 3	Col. 2.8–end
14	Zeph. 1.14–2.3	Col. 3.1–17
15	Zeph. 3	Col. 3.18–4.18
16	Haggai 2.1–9	1 Thess. 1
17	Zech. 1.1–17	1 Thess. 2
18 *St Luke*	Isa. 55	1 Thess. 3
19	Zech. 3	1 Thess. 4
20	Zech. 5	1 Thess. 5
21	Zech. 7	2 Thess. 1
22	Zech. 8.14–end	2 Thess. 2
23	Zech. 10	2 Thess. 3
24	Zech. 12	1 Tim. 1.1–17
25	Zech. 14	1 Tim. 1.18–2.15
26	Mal. 2	1 Tim. 3
27	Mal. 3.13–4.6	1 Tim. 4
28 *St Simon & St Jude*	Isa. 28.9–16	1 Tim. 5
29	Wisdom 2	1 Tim. 6
30	Wisdom 6.1–21	2 Tim. 1
31	Wisdom 7.15–end	2 Tim. 2

Readings for Daily Evening Prayer

OCTOBER	First Lesson	Second Lesson
1	Amos 4.4–end	Luke 5.1–16
2	Amos 5.18–6.8	Luke 5.17–end
3	Amos 8	Luke 6.1–19
4	Obadiah	Luke 6.20–end
5	Jonah 2	Luke 7.1–23
6	Jonah 4	Luke 7.24–end
7	Micah 2	Luke 8.1–25
8	Micah 4	Luke 8.26–end
9	Micah 6	Luke 9.1–27
10	Nahum 1	Luke 9.28–50
11	Nahum 3	Luke 9.51–10.16
12	Hab. 2	Luke 10.17–end
13	Zeph 1.1–13	Luke 11.1–28
14	Zeph. 2.4–end	Luke 11.29–end
15	Haggai 1	Luke 12.1–34
16	Haggai 2.10–end	Luke 12.35–end
17	Zech. 1.18–2.13	Luke 13.1–17
18 *St Luke*	Ecclus. 38.1–14	Luke 13.18–end
19	Zech. 4	Luke 14.1–24
20	Zech. 6	Luke 14.25–15.10
21	Zech. 8.1–13	Luke 15.11–end
22	Zech. 9.9–end	Luke 16
23	Zech. 11	Luke 17.1–19
24	Zech. 13	Luke 17.20–end
25	Mal. 1	Luke 18.1–30
26	Mal. 3.1–12	Luke 18.31–19.10
27	Wisdom 1	Luke 19.11–27
28 *St Simon & St Jude*	Jer. 3.12–18	Luke 19.28–end
29	Wisdom 4.7–end	Luke 20.1–26
30	Wisdom 6.22–7.14	Luke 20.27–21.4
31	Wisdom 8.1–18	Luke 21.5–end

Readings for Daily Morning Prayer

NOVEMBER	First Lesson	Second Lesson
1 *All Saints' Day*	Wisdom 3.1–9	Heb. 11.32–12.6
2	Wisdom 9	2 Tim. 3
3	Wisdom 11.15–12.2	2 Tim. 4
4	Ecclus. 1.1–13	Titus 1
5	Ecclus. 3.17–29	Titus 2
6	Ecclus. 5	Titus 3
7	Ecclus. 10.18–end	Philemon
8	Ecclus. 15.9–end	Heb. 1
9	Ecclus. 18.1–14	Heb. 2–3.6
10	Ecclus. 19.13–end	Heb. 3.7–4.13
11	Ecclus. 24.1–23	Heb. 4.14–5.14
12	Ecclus. 33.7–22	Heb. 6
13	Ecclus. 35	Heb. 7
14	Ecclus. 39.1–12	Heb. 8
15	Ecclus. 41.1–13	Heb. 9
16	Ecclus. 44.1–15	Heb. 10.1–18
17	Ecclus. 51.1–9	Heb. 10.19–end
18	Baruch 4.36–5.9	Heb. 11.1–16
19	Isa. 1.21–end	Heb. 11.17–end
20	Isa. 3.1–15	Heb. 12
21	Isa. 5.1–17	Heb. 13
22	Isa. 6	James 1
23	Isa. 8.5–17	James 2
24	Isa. 9.8–10.4	James 3
25	Isa. 10.20–end	James 4
26	Isa. 11.10–end	James 5
27	Isa. 13	1 Peter 1.1–21
28	Isa. 17	1 Peter 1.22–2.10
29	Isa. 19.1–15	1 Peter 2.11–3.7
30 *St Andrew, Ap*	Isa. 54	John 1.35–42

Readings for Daily Evening Prayer

NOVEMBER	First Lesson	Second Lesson
1 *All Saints' Day*	Wisdom 5.1–16	Rev. 19.1–16
2	Wisdom 11.1–14	Luke 22.1–30
3	Wisdom 17	Luke 22.31–53
4	Ecclus. 2	Luke 22.54–end
5	Ecclus. 4.10–end	Luke 23.1–25
6	Ecclus. 7.27–end	Luke 23.26–49
7	Ecclus. 14.1–19	Luke 23.50–24.12
8	Ecclus. 16.17–end	Luke 24.13–end
9	Ecclus. 18.15–end	John 1.1–28
10	Ecclus. 22.6–23	John 1.29–end
11	Ecclus. 24.24–end	John 2
12	Ecclus. 34.15–end	John 3.1–21
13	Ecclus. 37.8–18	John 3.22–end
14	Ecclus. 39.13–end	John 4.1–30
15	Ecclus. 42.15–end	John 4.31–end
16	Ecclus. 50.1–24	John 5.1–23
17	Baruch 4.1–20	John 5.24–end
18	Isa. 1.1–20	John 6.1–21
19	Isa. 2	John 6.22–40
20	Isa. 4.2–end	John 6.41–end
21	Isa. 5.18–end	John 7.1–24
22	Isa. 7.1–16	John 7.25–end
23	Isa. 8.18–9.7	John 8.1–30
24	Isa. 10.5–19	John 8.31–end
25	Isa. 11.1–9	John 9.1–38
26	Isa. 12	John 9.39–10.21
27	Isa. 14.1–23	John 10.22–end
28	Isa. 18	John 11.1–16
29	Isa. 19.16–end	John 11.17–46
30 *St Andrew, Ap*	Isa. 65.1–16	John 12.20–41

Readings for Daily Morning Prayer

DECEMBER		First Lesson	Second Lesson
1		Isa. 21.1–12	1 Peter 3.8–4.6
2		Isa. 22.15–end	1 Peter 4.7–end
3		Isa. 24	1 Peter 5
4		Isa. 26.1–19	2 Peter 1
5		Isa. 28.1–13	2 Peter 2
6		Isa. 29.1–8	2 Peter 3
7		Isa. 30.1–17	1 John 1
8		Isa. 31	1 John 2.1–14
9		Isa. 33	1 John 2.15–end
10		Isa. 35	1 John 3.1–15
11		Isa. 40.12–end	1 John 3.16–4.6
12		Isa. 41.17–end	1 John 4.7–end
13		Isa. 42.18–43.7	1 John 5
14		Isa. 44.1–20	2 John
15		Isa. 45.8–end	3 John
16		Isa. 47	Jude
17		Isa. 49.1–12	Rev. 1
18		Isa. 50	Rev. 2.18–3.6
19		Isa. 51.9–end	Rev. 4
20		Isa. 52.13–53.12	Rev. 6
21	*St Thomas, Ap*	Job 42.1–6	John 20.19–23
22		Isa. 55	Rev. 8
23		Isa. 57	Rev. 11
24		Isa. 59	Rev. 14
25	*Christmas Day*	Isa. 9.1–7	Luke 2.1–14
26	*St Stephen, M*	Gen. 4.1–10	Acts 6
27	*St John, Evang*	Exod. 33.9–end	John 13.23–35
28	*Innocents' Day*	Jer. 31.1–17	Rev. 16
29		Isa. 61	Rev. 19.1–10
30		Isa. 63	Rev. 20
31		Isa. 65.8–end	Rev. 21.15–22.5

Readings for Daily Evening Prayer

DECEMBER		First Lesson	Second Lesson
1		Isa. 22.1–14	John 11.47–12.19
2		Isa. 23	John 12.20–end
3		Isa. 25	John 13.1–20
4		Isa. 26.20–27.13	John 13.21–end
5		Isa. 28.14–end	John 14
6		Isa. 29.9–end	John 15
7		Isa. 30.18–end	John 16.1–15
8		Isa. 32	John 16.16–end
9		Isa. 34	John 17
10		Isa. 40.1–11	John 18.1–27
11		Isa. 41.1–16	John 18.28–end
12		Isa. 42.1–17	John 19.1–24
13		Isa. 43.8–end	John 19.25–end
14		Isa. 44.21–45.7	John 20.1–18
15		Isa. 46	John 20.19–end
16		Isa. 48	John 21
17		Isa. 49.13–end	Rev. 2.1–17
18		Isa. 51.1–8	Rev. 3.7–end
19		Isa. 52.1–12	Rev. 5
20		Isa. 54	Rev. 7
21	*St Thomas, Ap*	Isa. 35	John 14.1–7
22		Isa. 56	Rev. 10
23		Isa. 58	Rev. 12
24		Isa. 60	Rev. 15
25	*Christmas Day*	Isa. 7.10–16	Titus 3.4–8
26	*St Stephen, M*	2 Chron. 24.15–22	Acts 8.1–8
27	*St John, Evang*	Isa. 6	Rev. 1
28	*Innocents' Day*	Baruch 4.21–30	Rev. 18
29		Isa. 62	Rev. 19.11–end
30		Isa. 64–65.7	Rev. 21.1–14
31		Isa. 66	Rev. 22.6–end

Ash Wednesday

Readings for morning prayer

First Lesson	Second Lesson
Dan. 9.3–6,17–19	1 Tim. 6.6–19

Readings for evening prayer

First Lesson	Second Lesson
Isa. 1.10–18	Luke 15.11–32

Good Friday

Readings for morning prayer

First Lesson	Second Lesson
Lam. 5.15–end	John 18

Readings for evening prayer

First Lesson	Second Lesson
Gen. 22.1–18	John 19.38–end

Easter Day

Readings for morning prayer

First Lesson	Second Lesson
Exod. 14.10–18,26–15.2	Rev. 15.2–4

Readings for evening prayer

First Lesson	Second Lesson
Song of Sol. 3.2–5;8.6–7	John 20.11–18

Ascension Day

Readings for morning prayer

First Lesson	Second Lesson
Isa. 52.7–15	Heb. 7.[11–25] 26–28

Readings for evening prayer

First Lesson	Second Lesson
2 Kings 2.1–15	Rev. 5

Day of Pentecost

Readings for morning prayer

First Lesson	Second Lesson
Gen. 11.1–9	Acts 10.34–48

Readings for evening prayer

First Lesson	Second Lesson
Num. 11.24–30	Acts 2.14–21[22–38]

Trinity Sunday

Readings for morning prayer

First Lesson	Second Lesson
Exod. 3.1–6,13–15	John 17.1–11

Readings for evening prayer

First Lesson	Second Lesson
Isa. 40.12–17,27–31	John 16.5–15

Collects for Sundays and Principal Holy Days

The First Sunday of Christmas

Almighty God,
who wonderfully created us in your own image
and yet more wonderfully restored us
through your Son Jesus Christ:
grant that, as he came to share in our humanity,
so we may share the life of his divinity;
who is alive and reigns with you,
in the unity of the Holy Spirit,
one God, now and for ever.

The Second Sunday of Christmas

Almighty God,
in the birth of your Son
you have poured on us the new light of your incarnate Word,
and shown us the fullness of your love:
help us to walk in this light and dwell in his love
that we may know the fullness of his joy;
who is alive and reigns with you,
in the unity of the Holy Spirit,
one God, now and for ever.

The Epiphany

O God,
who by the leading of a star
manifested your only Son to the peoples of the earth:
mercifully grant that we,
who know you now by faith,
may at last behold your glory face to face;
through Jesus Christ your Son our Lord,
who is alive and reigns with you,
in the unity of the Holy Spirit,
one God, now and for ever.

The Baptism of Christ
The First Sunday of Epiphany

Eternal Father,
who at the baptism of Jesus
revealed him to be your Son,
anointing him with the Holy Spirit:
grant to us, who are born again by water and the Spirit,
that we may be faithful to our calling as your adopted
    children;
through Jesus Christ your Son our Lord,
who is alive and reigns with you,
in the unity of the Holy Spirit,
one God, now and for ever.

The Second Sunday of Epiphany

Almighty God,
in Christ you make all things new:
transform the poverty of our nature by the riches of your
    grace,
and in the renewal of our lives
make known your heavenly glory;
through Jesus Christ your Son our Lord,
who is alive and reigns with you,
in the unity of the Holy Spirit,
one God, now and for ever.

The Third Sunday of Epiphany

Almighty God,
whose Son revealed in signs and miracles
the wonder of your saving presence:
renew your people with your heavenly grace,
and in all our weakness
sustain us by your mighty power;
through Jesus Christ your Son our Lord,
who is alive and reigns with you,
in the unity of the Holy Spirit,
one God, now and for ever.

The Fourth Sunday of Epiphany

God our creator,
who in the beginning
commanded the light to shine out of darkness:
we pray that the light of the glorious gospel of Christ
may dispel the darkness of ignorance and unbelief,
shine into the hearts of all your people,
and reveal the knowledge of your glory
    in the face of Jesus Christ your Son our Lord,
who is alive and reigns with you,
in the unity of the Holy Spirit,
one God, now and for ever.

The Presentation of Christ in the Temple

Almighty and ever-living God,
clothed in majesty,
whose beloved Son was this day presented in the Temple,
in the substance of our flesh:
grant that we may be presented to you
with pure and clean hearts,
by your Son Jesus Christ our Lord,
who is alive and reigns with you,
in the unity of the Holy Spirit,
one God, now and for ever.

The Fifth Sunday before Lent

Almighty God,
by whose grace alone we are accepted
    and called to your service:
strengthen us by your Holy Spirit
and make us worthy of our calling;
through Jesus Christ your Son our Lord,
who is alive and reigns with you,
in the unity of the Holy Spirit,
one God, now and for ever.

The Fourth Sunday before Lent

O God,
you know us to be set
in the midst of so many and great dangers,
that by reason of the frailty of our nature
we cannot always stand upright:
grant to us such strength and protection
as may support us in all dangers
and carry us through all temptations;
through Jesus Christ your Son our Lord,
who is alive and reigns with you,
in the unity of the Holy Spirit,
one God, now and for ever.

The Third Sunday before Lent

Almighty God,
who alone can bring order
to the unruly wills and passions of sinful humanity:
give your people grace
so to love what you command
and to desire what you promise;
that, among the many changes of the world,
our hearts may surely there be fixed
where true joys are to be found;
through Jesus Christ your Son our Lord,
who is alive and reigns with you,
in the unity of the Holy Spirit,
one God, now and for ever.

The Second Sunday before Lent

Almighty God,
you have created the heavens and the earth
and made us in your own image:
teach us to discern your hand in all your works
and your likeness in all your children;
through Jesus Christ your Son our Lord,
who with you and the Holy Spirit reigns supreme over all
    things,
now and for ever.

The Sunday next before Lent

Almighty Father,
whose Son was revealed in majesty
before he suffered death upon the cross:
give us grace to perceive his glory,
that we may be strengthened to suffer with him
and be changed into his likeness, from glory to glory;
who is alive and reigns with you,
in the unity of the Holy Spirit,
one God, now and for ever.

Ash Wednesday

Almighty and everlasting God,
you hate nothing that you have made
and forgive the sins of all those who are penitent:
create and make in us new and contrite hearts
that we, worthily lamenting our sins
and acknowledging out wretchedness,
may receive from you, the God of all mercy,
perfect remission and forgiveness;
through Jesus Christ your Son our Lord,
who is alive and reigns with you,
in the unity of the Holy Spirit,
one God, now and for ever.

The First Sunday of Lent

Almighty God,
whose Son Jesus Christ fasted forty days in the wilderness,
and was tempted as we are, yet without sin:
give us grace to discipline ourselves in obedience to your
    Spirit;
and, as you know our weakness,
so may we know your power to save;
through Jesus Christ your Son our Lord,
who is alive and reigns with you,
in the unity of the Holy Spirit,
one God, now and for ever.

The Second Sunday of Lent

Almighty God,
you show to those who are in error the light of your truth,
that they may return to the way of righteousness:
grant to all those who are admitted
    into the fellowship of Christ's religion,
that they may reject those things
    that are contrary to their profession,
and follow all such things as are agreeable to the same;
through our Lord Jesus Christ,
who is alive and reigns with you,
in the unity of the Holy Spirit,
one God, now and for ever.

The Third Sunday of Lent

Almighty God,
whose most dear Son went not up to joy but first he suffered
    pain,
and entered not into glory before he was crucified:
mercifully grant that we, walking in the way of the cross,
may find it none other than the way of life and peace;
through Jesus Christ your Son our Lord,
who is alive and reigns with you,
in the unity of the Holy Spirit,
one God, now and for ever.

The Fourth Sunday of Lent

Merciful Lord,
absolve your people from their offences,
that through your bountiful goodness
we may all be delivered from the chains of those sins
which by our frailty we have committed;
grant this, heavenly Father,
for Jesus Christ's sake, our blessed Lord and Saviour,
who is alive and reigns with you,
in the unity of the Holy Spirit,
one God, now and for ever.

The Fifth Sunday of Lent

Most merciful God,
who by the death and resurrection of your Son Jesus Christ
delivered and saved the world:
grant that by faith in him who suffered on the cross,
we may triumph in the power of his victory;
through Jesus Christ your Son our Lord,
who is alive and reigns with you,
in the unity of the Holy Spirit,
one God, now and for ever.

Palm Sunday

Almighty and everlasting God,
who in your tender love towards the human race
    sent your Son our Saviour Jesus Christ
to take upon him our flesh
and to suffer death upon the cross:
grant that we may follow the example of his patience and
    humility,
and also be made partakers of his resurrection;
through Jesus Christ your Son our Lord,
who is alive and reigns with you,
in the unity of the Holy Spirit,
one God, now and for ever.

Maundy Thursday

God our Father,
you have invited us to share in the supper
which your Son gave to his Church
to proclaim his death until he comes:
may he nourish us by his presence,
and unite us in his love;
who is alive and reigns with you,
in the unity of the Holy Spirit,
one God, now and for ever.

Good Friday

Almighty Father,
look with mercy on this your family
for which our Lord Jesus Christ was content to be betrayed
    and given up into the hands of sinners
    and to suffer death upon the cross;
who is alive and glorified with you and the Holy Spirit,
one God, now and for ever.

Easter Eve

Grant, Lord,
that we who are baptized into the death
    of your Son our Saviour Jesus Christ
may continually put to death our evil desires
    and be buried with him;
and that through the grave and gate of death
we may pass to our joyful resurrection;
through his merits,
who died and was buried and rose again for us,
your Son Jesus Christ our Lord.

Easter Day

Lord of all life and power,
who through the mighty resurrection of your Son
overcame the old order of sin and death
to make all things new in him:
grant that we, being dead to sin
and alive to you in Jesus Christ,
may reign with him in glory;
to whom with you and the Holy Spirit
be praise and honour, glory and might,
now and in all eternity.

The Second Sunday of Easter

Almighty Father,
you have given your only Son to die for our sins
and to rise again for our justification:
grant us so to put away the leaven of malice and wickedness
that we may always serve you
in pureness of living and truth;
through the merits of your Son Jesus Christ our Lord,
who is alive and reigns with you,
in the unity of the Holy Spirit,
one God, now and for ever.

The Third Sunday of Easter

Almighty Father,
who in your great mercy gladdened the disciples
    with the sight of the risen Lord:
give us such knowledge of his presence with us,
that we may be strengthened and sustained by his risen life
and serve you continually in righteousness and truth;
through Jesus Christ you Son our Lord,
who is alive and reigns with you,
in the unity of the Holy Spirit,
one God, now and for ever.

The Fourth Sunday of Easter

Almighty God,
whose Son Jesus Christ is the resurrection and the life:
raise us, who trust in him,
from the death of sin to the life of righteousness,
that we may seek those things which are above,
where he reigns with you
in the unity of the Holy Spirit,
one God, now and for ever.

The Fifth Sunday of Easter

Almighty God,
who through your only-begotten Son Jesus Christ
have overcome death and opened to us the gate of
    everlasting life:
grant that, as by your grace going before us
    you put into our minds good desires,
so by your continual help
we may bring them to good effect;
through Jesus Christ our risen Lord,
who is alive and reigns with you,
in the unity of the Holy Spirit,
one God, now and for ever.

The Sixth Sunday of Easter

God our redeemer,
you have delivered us from the power of darkness
and brought us into the kingdom of your Son:
grant, that as by his death he has recalled us to life,
so by his continual presence in us he may raise us
    to eternal joy;
through Jesus Christ our Lord,
who is alive and reigns with you,
in the unity of the Holy Spirit,
one God, now and for ever.

Ascension Day

Grant, we pray, Almighty God,
that as we believe your only-begotten Son our Lord Jesus
    Christ
to have ascended into the heavens,
so we in heart and mind may also ascend
and with him continually dwell;
who is alive and reigns with you,
in the unity of the Holy Spirit,
one God, now and for ever.

The Seventh Sunday of Easter
Sunday after Ascension Day

O God the King of Glory,
you have exalted your only Son Jesus Christ
with great triumph to your kingdom in heaven:
we beseech you, leave us not comfortless,
but send your Holy Spirit to strengthen us
and exalt us to the place where our Saviour Christ is gone
    before,
who is alive and reigns with you,
in the unity of the Holy Spirit,
one God, now and for ever.

Day of Pentecost
Whit Sunday

God, who as at this time
taught the hearts of your faithful people
by sending to them the light of your Holy Spirit:
grant us by the same Spirit
to have right judgement in all things
and evermore to rejoice in his holy comfort;
through the merits of Christ Jesus our Saviour,
who is alive and reigns with you,
in the unity of the Holy Spirit,
one God, now and for ever.

Trinity Sunday

Almighty and everlasting God,
you have given us your servants grace,
by the confession of a true faith,
to acknowledge the glory of the eternal Trinity
and in the power of the divine majesty to worship the Unity:
keep us steadfast in this faith,
that we may evermore be defended from all adversities;
through Jesus Christ your Son our Lord,
who is alive and reigns with you,
in the unity of the Holy Spirit,
one God, now and for ever.

The First Sunday after Trinity

O God,
the strength of all those who put their trust in you,
mercifully accept our prayers
and, because through the weakness of our mortal nature
we can do no good thing without you,
grant us the help of your grace,
and in the keeping of your commandments
we may please you both in will and deed;
through Jesus Christ your Son our Lord,
who is alive and reigns with you,
in the unity of the Holy Spirit,
one God, now and for ever.

The Second Sunday after Trinity

Lord, you have taught us
that all our doings without love are nothing worth:
send your Holy Spirit
and pour into our hearts that most excellent gift of love,
the true bond of peace and of all virtues,
without which whoever lives is counted dead before you.
Grant this for your only Son Jesus Christ's sake,
who is alive and reigns with you,
in the unity of the Holy Spirit,
one God, now and for ever.

The Third Sunday after Trinity

Almighty God,
you have broken the tyranny of sin
and have sent the Spirit of your Son into our hearts
    whereby we call you Father:
give us grace to dedicate our freedom to your service,
that we and all creation may be brought
    to the glorious liberty of the children of God;
through Jesus Christ your Son our Lord,
who is alive and reigns with you,
in the unity of the Holy Spirit,
one God, now and for ever.

The Fourth Sunday after Trinity

O God, the protector of all who trust in you,
without whom nothing is strong, nothing is holy:
increase and multiply upon us your mercy;
that with you as our ruler and guide
we may so pass through things temporal
that we lose not our hold on things eternal;
grant this, heavenly Father,
for our Lord Jesus Christ's sake,
who is alive and reigns with you,
in the unity of the Holy Spirit,
one God, now and for ever.

The Fifth Sunday after Trinity

Almighty and everlasting God,
by whose Spirit the whole body of the Church
    is governed and sanctified:
hear our prayer which we offer for all your faithful people,
that in their vocation and ministry
they may serve you in holiness and truth
to the glory of your name;
through our Lord and Saviour Jesus Christ,
who is alive and reigns with you,
in the unity of the Holy Spirit,
one God, now and for ever.

The Sixth Sunday after Trinity

Merciful God,
you have prepared for those who love you
such good things as pass our understanding:
pour into our hearts such love toward you
that we, loving you in all things and above all things,
may obtain your promises,
which exceed all that we can desire;
through Jesus Christ our Lord,
who is alive and reigns with you,
in the unity of the Holy Spirit,
one God, now and for ever.

The Seventh Sunday after Trinity

Lord of all power and might,
the author and giver of all good things:
graft in our hearts the love of your name,
increase in us true religion,
nourish us with all goodness,
and of your great mercy keep us in the same;
through Jesus Christ your Son our Lord,
who is alive and reigns with you,
in the unity of the Holy Spirit,
one God, now and for ever.

The Eighth Sunday after Trinity

Almighty Lord and everlasting God,
we beseech you to direct, sanctify and govern
    both our hearts and bodies
in the ways of your laws
    and the works of your commandments;
that through your most mighty protection, both here
    and ever,
we may be preserved in body and soul;
through our Lord and Saviour Jesus Christ,
who is alive and reigns with you,
in the unity of the Holy Spirit,
one God, now and for ever.

The Ninth Sunday after Trinity

Almighty God,
who sent your Holy Spirit
to be the life and light of your Church:
open our hearts to the riches of his grace,
that we may bring forth the fruit of the Spirit
in love and joy and peace;
through Jesus Christ your Son our Lord,
who is alive and reigns with you,
in the unity of the Holy Spirit,
one God, now and for ever.

The Tenth Sunday after Trinity

Let your merciful ears, O Lord,
be open to the prayers of your humble servants;
and that they may obtain their petitions
make them to ask such things as shall please you;
through Jesus Christ your Son our Lord,
who is alive and reigns with you,
in the unity of the Holy Spirit,
one God, now and for ever.

The Eleventh Sunday after Trinity

O God, you declare your Almighty power
most chiefly in showing mercy and pity:
mercifully grant to us such a measure of your grace,
that we, running the way of your commandments,
may receive your gracious promises,
and be made partakers of your heavenly treasure;
through Jesus Christ your Son our Lord,
who is alive and reigns with you,
in the unity of the Holy Spirit,
one God, now and for ever.

The Twelfth Sunday after Trinity

Almighty and everlasting God,
you are always more ready to hear than we to pray
and to give more than either we desire or deserve:
pour down upon us the abundance of your mercy,
forgiving us those things of which our conscience is afraid
and giving us those good things
    which we are not worthy to ask
but through the merits and mediation
of Jesus Christ your Son our Lord,
who is alive and reigns with you,
in the unity of the Holy Spirit,
one God, now and for ever.

The Thirteenth Sunday after Trinity

Almighty God,
who called your Church to bear witness
that you were in Christ reconciling the world to yourself:
help us to proclaim the good news of your love,
that all who hear it may be drawn to you;
through him who was lifted up on the cross,
and reigns with you in the unity of the Holy Spirit,
one God, now and for ever.

The Fourteenth Sunday after Trinity

Almighty God,
whose only Son has opened for us
a new and living way into your presence:
give us pure hearts and steadfast wills
to worship you in spirit and in truth;
through Jesus Christ your Son our Lord,
who is alive and reigns with you,
in the unity of the Holy Spirit,
one God, now and for ever.

The Fifteenth Sunday after Trinity

God, who in generous mercy sent the Holy Spirit
   upon your Church in the burning fire of your love:
grant that your people may be fervent
   in the fellowship of the gospel
that, always abiding in you,
they may be found steadfast in faith and active in service;
through Jesus Christ our Lord,
who is alive and reigns with you,
in the unity of the Holy Spirit,
one God, now and for ever.

The Sixteenth Sunday after Trinity

O Lord, we beseech you mercifully to hear the prayers
   of your people who call upon you;
and grant that they may both perceive and know
   what things they ought to do,
and also may have grace and power faithfully to fulfil them;
through Jesus Christ your Son our Lord,
who is alive and reigns with you,
in the unity of the Holy Spirit,
one God, now and for ever.

The Seventeenth Sunday after Trinity

Almighty God,
you have made us for yourself,
and our hearts are restless till they find their rest in you:
pour your love into our hearts and draw us to yourself,
and so bring us at last to your heavenly city
where we shall see you face to face;
through Jesus Christ your Son our Lord,
who is alive and reigns with you,
in the unity of the Holy Spirit,
one God, now and for ever.

The Eighteenth Sunday after Trinity

Almighty and everlasting God,
increase in us your gift of faith
that, forsaking what lies behind
and reaching out to that which is before,
we may run the way of your commandments
and win the crown of everlasting joy;
through Jesus Christ your Son our Lord,
who is alive and reigns with you,
in the unity of the Holy Spirit,
one God, now and for ever.

The Nineteenth Sunday after Trinity

O God, forasmuch as without you
we are not able to please you;
mercifully grant that your Holy Spirit
may in all things direct and rule our hearts;
through Jesus Christ your Son our Lord.
who is alive and reigns with you,
in the unity of the Holy Spirit,
one God, now and for ever.

The Twentieth Sunday after Trinity

God, the giver of life,
whose Holy Spirit wells up within your Church:
by the Spirit's gifts equip us to live the gospel of Christ
    and make us eager to do your will,
that we may share with the whole creation
    the joys of eternal life;
through Jesus Christ your Son our Lord,
who is alive and reigns with you,
in the unity of the Holy Spirit,
one God, now and for ever.

The Twenty-first Sunday after Trinity

Grant, we beseech you, merciful Lord,
to your faithful people pardon and peace,
that they may be cleansed from all their sins
and serve you with a quiet mind;
through Jesus Christ your Son our Lord,
who is alive and reigns with you,
in the unity of the Holy Spirit,
one God, now and for ever.

The Last Sunday after Trinity

Blessed Lord,
who caused all holy Scriptures to be written for our learning:
help us to hear them,
to read, mark, learn and inwardly digest them
that, through patience, and the comfort of your holy word,
we may embrace and for ever hold fast
   the hope of everlasting life,
which you have given us in our Saviour Jesus Christ,
who is alive and reigns with you,
in the unity of the Holy Spirit,
one God, now and for ever.

The Fourth Sunday before Advent

Almighty and eternal God,
you have kindled the flame of love
   in the hearts of the saints:
grant to us the same faith and power of love,
that, as we rejoice in their triumphs,
we may be sustained by their example and fellowship;
through Jesus Christ your Son our Lord,
who is alive and reigns with you,
in the unity of the Holy Spirit,
one God, now and for ever.

The Third Sunday before Advent

Almighty Father,
whose will is to restore all things
in your beloved Son, the king of all:
govern the hearts and minds of those in authority,
and bring the families of the nations,
divided and torn apart by the ravages of sin,
to be subject to his just and gentle rule;
who is alive and reigns with you
in the unity of the Holy Spirit,
one God, now and for ever.

The Second Sunday before Advent

Heavenly Father,
whose blessed Son was revealed
    to destroy the works of the devil
and make us the children of God and heirs of eternal life:
grant that we, having this hope,
may purify ourselves even as he is pure;
that when he shall appear in power and great glory
we may be made like him in his eternal and glorious
    kingdom;
where he is alive and reigns with you,
in the unity of the Holy Spirit,
one God, now and for ever.

The Apostles' Creed

I believe in God, the Father Almighty,
creator of heaven and earth.

I believe in Jesus Christ, his only Son, our Lord,
who was conceived by the Holy Spirit,
born of the Virgin Mary,
suffered under Pontius Pilate,
was crucified, died, and was buried;
he descended to the dead.
On the third day he rose again;
he ascended into heaven,
he is seated at the right hand of the Father,
and he will come to judge the living and the dead.

I believe in the Holy Spirit,
the holy catholic Church,
the communion of saints,
the forgiveness of sins,
the resurrection of the body,
and the life everlasting.
Amen.